Stop Surviving Start Fighting

Jazz Thornton

16pt

Read How You Want
LARGE PRINT BOOKS, BRAILLE & DAISY

Copyright Page from the Original Book

TABLE OF CONTENTS

Introduction   v

Section One: CORE BELIEFS   1

CHAPTER ONE: The conversation   1

CHAPTER TWO: Identifying the enemy   8

CHAPTER THREE: Going back to the start   14

CHAPTER FOUR: Extreme reactions   25

CHAPTER FIVE: Running away   32

CHAPTER SIX: Downward spiral   45

CHAPTER SEVEN: Crisis   53

CHAPTER EIGHT: Psych ward   64

CHAPTER NINE: Breaking the beliefs   73

CHAPTER TEN: Speaking hope   80

Section Two: FEARS   90

CHAPTER ELEVEN: Abandonment   90

CHAPTER TWELVE: Crisis response   100

CHAPTER THIRTEEN: Cast aside   112

CHAPTER FOURTEEN: Developed fear   123

CHAPTER FIFTEEN: Fear of three   133

CHAPTER SIXTEEN: Fight the fears   145

CHAPTER SEVENTEEN: Straight talking   154

CHAPTER EIGHTEEN: 'Attention-seeker'   165

CHAPTER NINETEEN: Changing the script   177

Section Three: ENGAGE   184

CHAPTER TWENTY: The battle   184

CHAPTER TWENTY-ONE: Phases of battle   192

CHAPTER TWENTY-TWO: Failure to engage   201

CHAPTER TWENTY-THREE: Behind the fear   212

CHAPTER TWENTY-FOUR: Breakthrough   222

CHAPTER TWENTY-FIVE: 'Dear Suicidal Me'   230

CHAPTER TWENTY-SIX: Strengths   239

CHAPTER TWENTY-SEVEN: The power of decisions   252

Section Four: SAVIOUR   263

CHAPTER TWENTY-EIGHT: Saviour?   263
CHAPTER TWENTY-NINE: Jessica's Tree   274
CHAPTER THIRTY: What's our responsibility?   285
Section Five: FORGIVENES   296
CHAPTER THIRTY-ONE: Why forgiveness is important 296
CHAPTER THIRTY-TWO: The hardest to forgive   305
CHAPTER THIRTY-THREE: Forgiving yourself   315
Section Six: DREAM   328
CHAPTER THIRTY-FOUR: The importance of dreaming 328
CHAPTER THIRTY-FIVE: What stops us dreaming   339
CHAPTER THIRTY-SIX: 'Dear Suicidal Me' 2   350
CHAPTER THIRTY-SEVEN: Dream turned reality   359
Acknowledgements   379
Where to get help   383

This book is dedicated to every person who is battling mental illness. To every person who is fighting something that people cannot see—your illness is not your identity and it is possible to change the script of your life. I hope this book not only inspires you, but also equips you for how you can engage in your own fight.

You are not alone, there is always hope.

Jazz x

'Jazz writes with such honesty, courage and insight. This book is a must, not just for those with mental illness, but for all of humanity. Jazz reminds us through her own inspirational story that we all have a part to play to keep each other, as well as ourselves, fighting and not just surviving. I am truly inspired by Jazz's book—it has given me new hope for the future. Thanks Jazz for sharing yourself with us so vulnerably. I know that by writing your story with immense bravery and candour you will impact not only the world around you today but many generations to come.'
—*Jonny Benjamin MBE*
British mental health campaigner, writer, filmmaker & public speaker

'Jazz's inspiring story will provide hope to many who are struggling to believe there is a way out of the darkness and confusion that comes with mental health challenges. Her life is a testimony to hope, and a radical call to action for more support to be made available for those who need it.'
—*Elisha London*

Founder and CEO of United for Global Mental Health

The information contained in this book is of a general nature only and not a substitute for professional medical advice. If you wish to make any use of information in this book relating to your health, you should first consider its appropriateness to your situation and obtain advice from a medical professional.

Dear Reader,

Let me first say thank you. Thank you for choosing to pick up this book — whether it be for you or for a friend or family member, it is my hope that this book may be a tool to help create change. This book does talk about suicide, sexual abuse and a few other hard topics, so please, read at your own pace and take breaks. There is a list of helplines at the back. Please go there and use them any time you need to.

You are not alone and no matter what you are facing, there is always hope.

All my love,

Jazz x

Introduction

The first time I tried to kill myself, I was just 12 years old. I sat in my bedroom at home, while my mum watched TV a few metres away through the wall. I was overwhelmed by feelings of hopelessness. I felt worthless and like I was a burden to everyone who knew me.

As I started to feel dizzy and sick from what I'd done, I freaked out. I ran into my mum's room and told her what had happened. And so that also became the first time I had to be taken to hospital to be treated for the effects of attempting to take my life.

You might be thinking I am an extreme case. But, sadly, that's not true. I was just an average Kiwi kid, growing up in a single-parent family in a small town. I faced the same challenges many of our children face—bullying, fatherlessness, lack of self-confidence. Every year in New Zealand, half a dozen or more kids aged under 15 take their own lives—and there will be many more than that who attempt it, and even more again who seriously contemplate it. It's a fact that New Zealand has one of the worst youth-suicide rates in the developed world. It's not just young people, either—our overall recorded suicide rate for 2018–19 was the highest since records began.

I began this introduction by saying 'the first time I tried to kill myself'. Unfortunately, it was far from the last. Over the next eight years, I would try to take my life another 13 times—coming pretty close a few times. I've been found unconscious, talked down by police, physically restrained, hospitalised, put in a psychiatric hospital under a legal order, and still I tried again and again to take my life.

It wasn't until I was 20 years old that I finally realised that there had to be another way, and that I was the only person who could truly break this cycle. I realised I had to stop surviving and start fighting.

From that point, I made it my mission to find out what it was that was driving me to feel the way I felt—not just what had happened to me in my life's journey, but how I had reacted to it and made it part of what I believed about myself, making me feel like I didn't deserve to be alive. It wasn't an easy thing to do, but with the love and support of people who really cared about me, I have put my life back together.

I have gone from being too mentally unwell to hold down a job, home or relationship to being the youngest person to be awarded funding to make a documentary through the Doc Edge scheme. With my good friend and co-founder Genevieve Mora, I have set up a charity, Voices of Hope, which aims to provide inspiration, encouragement and resources to young people struggling with mental-health issues. I have become a public speaker, travelling all over New Zealand and the world telling the story of my journey, and spreading a message of hope. I've even met with royalty working in the field of mental health.

When I was in high school, I remember having inspirational speakers come in and talk to us about what they had achieved in their lives. At the time they were speaking, I would think, 'Wow, that's amazing! But how did they get to where they are now?' I might be inspired at the time, but then when my own life went sideways again I would find myself falling into my old habits and patterns and merely struggling to stay alive. I began to realise that inspirational stories are great in terms of giving people a destination to aim for, but they often skip over the journey—the story of the fight, of *how* that person got to where they are.

This book *is* about that journey—my journey—of how I went from suicidal to hopeful, including the good, the bad and the straight-up ugly. It's about how I came to be suicidal in the first place, and why I tried so many times to end my life during my teenage years. It's about how I decided to change, to engage in the battle with my mental health and to fight for my life. It's about what I found out along the way, and how I was able to turn my life around. It's about how I was able to take my newfound strength and use it to achieve my dreams.

It's about how an ordinary Kiwi kid, just like you or your child, can get to the point of wanting to end their own life—and how they can come back from that.

Most of all, it's about hope. I know what it's like to want to die, and to feel such deep despair that there doesn't seem to be any other way out. But I also know there is always hope. I am living proof.

Let me tell you my story.

Section One

CORE BELIEFS

CHAPTER ONE

The conversation

The idea of *Stop Surviving Start Fighting* came from a single conversation that changed my life—a conversation that took me from suicidal to hopeful, from brokenness to wholeness. This conversation happened after what turned out to be my final suicide attempt, when I was 20 years old.

I had been taken to hospital by the police following my suicide attempt, and admitted to the psychiatric ward. However, I'd tried to hurt myself again, even once I was in the psych ward, so I got moved back to the emergency department. I'd only recently been released after several months in the psych ward into a respite house, but

I'd been kicked out of there too, after trying to hurt myself. The mental-health crisis team decided that the psych ward wasn't working for me (I could have told them that!), and they suggested that they would move me into community care. Unfortunately they decided this at about 1.30a.m., and as I was released legally under the Mental Health Act, that meant I was able to just get up and leave. So I did. I got up and walked out of the hospital at about 2a.m. and spent the whole rest of the night walking around the streets of Auckland by myself.

I literally didn't have anywhere to go. I had next to nothing—no home, no job and no income, just my government benefit. I had become isolated from all my friends and felt like I had no one to turn to. However, as I was walking the streets of Auckland city, exhausted and broken, I realised that if I was going to keep on living I really couldn't do this alone.

Having a survival instinct is important, but surviving has never propelled anyone *through* a situation.

There was one person who I felt I could reach out to: my friend Esther. I had first met Esther when I saw the Revolution Tour, an anti-bullying roadshow, and then when I moved to Auckland when I was 16, I had found that we went to the same church. We had become close, and she had become one of the key people in my life. She had seen me at my worst, many times—watched me go through my pattern of becoming suicidal and ending up in hospital over and over again, while all the time I pretended to the rest of the world that I was OK. But over the past few months I had pushed her away, along with everyone else who I had become close to.

It took every bit of what little strength I had left in me to text Esther and admit that I was a mess again. I was so ashamed that I had gone in another circle, and that I had pushed people like her away, thinking I could do it by myself. It was like I was waving a little white flag and saying 'I have screwed up big-time—turns out I can't do this by myself after all...'

When Esther woke up and got my message, she replied saying she would be in the church office later that morning and that I should come and see her. As I began to walk up there, I was filled with anxiety, thinking over and over again how much I had messed up. I was a train wreck.

Esther was sitting in a little side room beside the main offices. I slowly stepped in with tears rolling down my face, feeling so ashamed that I had reached this point again. I sat next to her on the couch and just started ugly-crying.

Esther turned to me and asked, 'Jazz, why are you crying?' I looked up at her and said through my tears, 'I'm just so tired of fighting.'

What she said next went on to change—and ultimately save—my life.

'Jazz, what do you think the definition of fighting is? Because I don't think you are fighting—I think you are only surviving. It is only when you learn how to fight that the change you are longing to see is going to happen.'

'It is only when you learn how to fight that the change you are longing to see is going to happen.'

Something in her words sparked a fire in me. I remember thinking in that moment that if what she was saying was true—that I really had just been surviving this whole time, and that fighting might actually change something—then what I had to do was learn how to fight. For so long I had assumed that I was simply a lost cause and that nothing could 'fix me'. Little did I know that there was still so much that I hadn't actually tried. And if that was the case, then that meant there was still hope.

Later that day, the mental-health crisis team came and picked me up and took me to a respite house (the same one I had previously been kicked out of for trying to take my life there ... go figure!). As I unloaded my bags back into the room, I began thinking back on my conversation with Esther. I knew that I needed to start fighting, but I had no idea *where* to start. I decided to do what any self-respecting researcher would do: I googled the definitions of surviving and fighting, and here is what I found.

The definition of surviving was 'to continue to live or exist in hardship. Manage to keep going in difficult circumstances.'

As I read that, it hit me—maybe I had actually been just surviving all these years. I had been continuing to live in my hardship, and my behaviour, emotional responses and thought patterns had remained the same. Don't get me wrong: having a survival instinct is important—it is what keeps us going when times are tough—but surviving has never propelled anyone *through* a situation, and leaves you accepting the situation you are in.

Next, the definition of fighting was 'to engage in a battle or war, fight to overcome and destroy an adversary.' A little bit different from surviving, huh?

I felt as if I had been hit in the stomach. I had spent years complaining about how hard I was fighting, but according to this definition, I wasn't really fighting at all.

The very first thing that caught my eye about this definition was the word 'engage'—to *engage* in a battle or war. Looking at my own life, my story and my issues, had I actually been engaging in the battle? Had I been fighting to challenge and destroy my thinking, behaviours and emotional responses? Most definitely not. If I wanted to see change in my life, then I needed to learn how to stop surviving and start fighting.

CHAPTER TWO

Identifying the enemy

The very first thing I had to do to fight was to learn what I was fighting. If you don't know *what* you are fighting, it is impossible to know *how* to fight it.

I had spent so long thinking that I was fighting my suicidal tendencies, believing that if I could make myself stop feeling suicidal then I would be fine. However, I soon realised that I wasn't fighting my suicidal thoughts or my destructive patterns, I was fighting the beliefs that put me into that behavioural pattern—the beliefs that every few months would lead to actions that would see me in an emergency room, in a police station or in the psych ward.

I began to think back on the last 14 times I had tried to take my life to try and identify what emotions and thoughts were prominent. What did I believe—about myself and about other people—that led me to think I should kill myself? How had the things that had happened to me when I was younger led me to have this set of core beliefs that were governing my life—and making me want to end it?

Our internal belief system is shaped by all kinds of things. Different life experiences—both good and bad—as well as your culture, family, school and friends all play a part in forming the things you believe about yourself, from a very young age. For some, even a small incident can set off a long-term belief that we might struggle to identify and 'call out' later down the line.

Different life experiences—both good and bad—as well as your culture, family, school and friends all play a part in forming the things you believe about yourself.

A belief is something that we accept as true, sometimes without evidence. Our brain believes it is factual. Beliefs are powerful things—they determine how you see the world and the future, how you choose to act and protect yourself, how you navigate your way through life.

They form the foundations of all our relationships. Our beliefs also colour what we perceive others think about us. They inform our insecurities and also influence what we think we can and cannot achieve.

The majority of our beliefs are formed when we are kids, which means that sometimes the smallest of situations can trigger a series of untrue beliefs. You see, when we are young we are often unable to figure out what is true and what is a lie and so we take everything in as fact. When bad things happen, they make sense to a child's logic, which creates a lens through which the child sees the world.

As you grow older and you are exposed to more of the world, your core beliefs start to develop and grow. You now have a whole different world of people telling you things. The saying 'sticks and stones may break my bones but words will never hurt me' angers me so much and I believe it couldn't be further from the truth. If you spend a year telling a boy that he is useless, soon enough it is going to form a belief in him and he will start to see it as truth. I was bullied at school, and constantly being called disgusting, ugly and unwanted ensured that soon enough I saw these opinions as the truth about myself. Unlike the saying, the words *did* hurt me—in fact, they helped develop a warped identity that would tell me every day I didn't deserve to be here. **Beliefs are powerful things—they determine how you see the world, how you choose to act and protect yourself, how you navigate your way through life.**

Sometimes our beliefs are rooted so far back that we forget how they were formed and we only see their stems, which our brain interprets into fact. Let me tell you a little bit about my life up to this point, which I thought back on as I tried to unpick my core beliefs and where they had come from.

When I looked back over my life, I could see a sequence of events and experiences that had formed me into the person I was at that time—despairing, suicidal and in a cycle of self-harm that I could see no way out of. I had so many warped beliefs about myself that altered my behaviour as a teenager and launched me into a world of hurt.

Looking back, I could see that my earlier suicide attempts were often focused on external circumstances, such as being bullied, but my internal battle seemed to be based on the belief that 'everyone hates me'. As I got older, that had developed into a feeling that I was a complete burden to everyone around me. I had come to believe that simply by being alive, I was wasting people's time and energy. I genuinely believed that everyone would be better off without me here.

The saying 'sticks and stones may break my bones but words will never hurt me' angers me so much. It couldn't be further from the truth.

This was heavily supported by the next core belief I identified: that I was unlovable. I mean, if I couldn't love myself, then how could anyone else love me? I felt I could get love momentarily or short-term, especially at times of crisis, but I had come to believe that as soon as anyone got to know the 'real me' they would hate me.

Armed with these two core beliefs, is it any wonder that I tried so often to take my life? This was what I had to fight against if I was going to engage in the battle to turn my thinking and behaviour around and save my own life.

CHAPTER THREE

Going back to the start

Figuring out how these beliefs were formed was a long and hard process. I was so desperate to understand why I was the way I was, but for such a long time I hadn't been able to figure that out. I had come to believe it was just part of who I was. I had seen counsellors on and off since I was a kid, but to be honest I never trusted any of them long enough for them to explore why I felt this way. In fact, the majority of counsellors and health professionals whom I saw during my teenage years played into my belief that this was just who I was—they were all about trying to get me to modify my behaviour instead of helping to figure out why I thought and acted this way.

A couple of years earlier, I had tried to find out what might have happened in my childhood that had started me off down this path. I decided to submit a formal request to view my files from the government agency responsible for the wellbeing of children here in New Zealand, which at that time was called Child, Youth and Family Services (CYFS). I knew that they had files on me, because of something that had happened when I had first moved to Auckland when I was 16.

It was not long after I had arrived in the city, but it was the second place I had lived at. I found out that the people I had ended up living with were doing Class A drugs and some pretty major store robberies to fund their habit. I didn't really know what to do or how to get out of there, so I started recording some of my conversations with them, and after a few months went to the police. There was a seven-year-old girl in the house as well, so I really wanted to help get her out of that environment, too.

I think I knew that what was happening was wrong, because I was told I wasn't allowed to tell anyone about it, but it seemed more like a game than anything else.

When the police raided the house, they gave me and the young girl ten minutes to pack our belongings, then they drove us to the local CYFS office. While we were sitting in the waiting room and they were arranging for the seven-year-old to be looked after, I was told that I was too old now for the system (thankfully the systems have changed now!). The child protection worker said to me, 'I can see on our files that you have had a pretty hard childhood', and I remember sitting there stunned. I had no recollection of being involved with CYFS as a child, so knowing there was a written record of things that had happened to me took me by surprise. I knew that stuff had happened as a kid, but I never knew any of it was actually recorded.

I found out that I wasn't legally allowed to access my files until I was 18, however, so I had to wait two years until I could ask for them. It was always in the back of my mind though, so once I turned 18 I submitted the request online, stating that I wanted to try to understand what had happened to me as a kid. Then a couple of weeks later I got a call to say that I was able to go into the local office and collect my files.

I didn't have a car at this point, so I had to get on a bus and then walk up a large hill to get to the office. The whole journey there, I felt like my heart was going to beat out of my chest. I was so anxious. Part of me wanted to know, but I was also afraid of finding out what was in the files. My mind was running through all of the different scenarios, trying to imagine what could be in there.

I was forced to go on living in the silence of the things that had happened to me.

As I finally reached the office I stood outside for about five minutes, just staring up at the sign. Now I was finally able to get these files, I wasn't at all sure if I wanted to read them anymore. Eventually I plucked up the courage to open the door and walk up to the reception area.

The office was very clinical looking, but the receptionist was lovely. She asked me for my ID before disappearing around the corner to get my files. Ten minutes later she returned with a large brown envelope with my name on the front. As she handed it over to me, she said, 'I think you should read this with someone—it might be really hard.'

Her words stuck with me as I left. While I wanted to rip open the envelope right away, I knew that I should be wise and do what she said.

I decided to get in touch with one of my friends, Nic. Nic was the kids' pastor at Equippers Church, and I had spent the past six months working with her on the different kids' programmes the church ran. We had become quite close that year, to the point where I was often staying at her house with her family. She had became a key person that I turned to, and I knew that I could trust her.

Having previously worked in mental health, I always felt that Nic never judged me. She never saw me as an 'attention seeker' and she never disregarded my behaviour. She always chose to look beyond my issues and try to find out why I was struggling. So when the time came for me to read these files, I felt Nic was the right person to do this with.

I discussed it with her and we decided that Nic would read through the files first and then we would go through them together. Nic took them home and read through them, then the following week she picked me up and we drove back to her house to go through them together. As we walked into her house she said, 'So, I have put highlighter tabs on the areas that might be hard for you to read.' She pulled out the documents and they were covered in highlighter tabs. I felt my heart drop. Once again, I didn't know if I wanted to read the files. What if I don't want to know what happened anymore? What if it wasn't what I was after? What if it didn't give me an answer?

I think Nic could see me struggling. She added, 'I don't think you will remember a lot of this. There are a couple of different men mentioned in them. There is also an interview with you when you were three. Just take your time and stop if you need to.'

I took a deep breath and opened the first file. As I began to read the black-and-white pages, I felt tears rolling down my cheeks.

Jasmine has gone from bubbly and happy to dull and lacking emotion.

Suspicion of sexual abuse after mother found XXX XXXXX XXX XXXXXXXX on XXXXXXXXX XXXXXX. Mother asked Jasmine about it and XXX XXXX XXXX XXXXX XXX XXXX XXXXXXX XXX XXXX XXXXX.

Immediate action and investigation required.

(redacted due to personal information)

*

The man named in this part was someone who I had grown up with, someone who I had known pretty much all of my life. I always had one particular memory of this person, of us being in a white shed outside the back of his house. He grew sunflowers in the shed, so there was a whole lot of them on the shelves. I remember it being a nice day outside, I remember the smell of freshly cut grass and I remember walking into the shed with him. That was the shed he sexually abused me in. I didn't know any better and so I went along with it. After that it becomes a bit of a blur.

This memory was one that I had pushed to the very back of my mind. I had always remembered the shed, but chose to black out the rest. It wasn't until I read that line on the files that it all came rushing back to me.

In the rest of my files, I read of three different men who sexually abused me—three different men who blamed each other to hide their own wrongdoing. Three men who stole my innocence.

My recollection around this abuse is a mixture of very clear at times and pretty blurry at others, like the memory above. I think I knew that what was happening was wrong, because I was told I wasn't allowed to tell anyone about it, but it seemed more like a game than anything else. I didn't know any different. I didn't know that grown men should not be engaging in sexual behaviour with three-year-old girls. To me, it seemed totally normal.

One memory that stands out to me is when I was staying overnight at the house of one of the men in my files. I remember lying in what felt like a huge bed with this man, and he asked me if I wanted to play 'the up and down game'. I didn't really want to play it because I was tired and I missed my mum, but he said that if I loved him then I would play it with him. It felt like we were playing it forever, and then I suddenly threw up all over the bed. He got mad and ran out of the room to get a bucket and a new set of sheets. I don't know if I was genuinely sick, or if my body was reacting to the situation, but I am thankful to this day that I vomited because he didn't touch me for the rest of the night after that.

My experience of love and being kept safe by the people who loved me was warped and then shattered, instilling in me my belief of being unlovable.

In my files, I also read a transcript of an interview with me as a three-year-old. When I walked into the room for the interview, right away I said, 'He didn't hurt me. He really didn't, I promise.' The interviewer then noted, 'Why would Jasmine come in and say this right away? She has been coached.'

As a three-year-old girl, I was obviously being sexually abused, but nobody with any authority acted. Any investigations fell flat, as the people involved denied the allegations and then coached me to say nothing had happened. I didn't act scared of the perpetrators, probably because I didn't know that what they were doing was a serious crime. Today studies have shown that is completely normal behaviour for those who have been sexually abused, but back then it was considered evidence that nothing had happened. If I wasn't scared of them, I must be fine.

The only thing CYFS could do was put in place conditions that I wasn't allowed to see the men named in my files. While one of them left my life, the other two didn't, and I had to just go on living in the silence of the things that had happened to me. I had to live with the fear that if I made a fuss my whole family would break up and it would all be my fault, so I just had to pretend that nothing had happened.

I had seen anger from those around me following this investigation, and my little undeveloped brain must have gone, 'This is my fault. I am the reason that they are mad.' At that young age my experience of love and being kept safe by the people who loved me was warped and then shattered, instilling in me my belief of being unlovable.

When I had finished reading, I put the files down and cried. Nic moved over and sat beside me, and I leant into her and continued to cry. As hard as it was reading these files, I felt like I finally had a bit more clarity about what had happened to me as a child. It had helped to fill in a lot of blurry memories, and I felt for the first time I could start to try to close that chapter of my life. However, unfortunately it would be a few more years and a few more suicide attempts before I really began to address the effects of this abuse.

CHAPTER FOUR

Extreme reactions

Another interesting thing that my files had said was that my reactions to small events were huge:

The concern I have is the way Jazz reacts when she has done something wrong. If one of the children come and tell me Jazz hit them, I would find her hiding with her head down...

She had trouble in the bathroom once and couldn't wipe herself properly. Her reaction to it was extreme; she ran outside and was curled up in a ball, crying...

She does this even when small things have happened ... always acts like she expects something serious to happen and she uses bad language...

This was something I had continued to struggle with, throughout my childhood and particularly my teenage years, especially once my suicidal behaviour really ramped up. I always seemed to have the most extreme reactions to events, to take things really hard and get more upset about things than other people. Reading those files, it suddenly made sense to me why as a teenager my responses to small things were always so huge—I was responding like that little three-year-old abused girl, in the corner crying, with no one coming to help her.

I was responding like that little three-year-old abused girl, in the corner crying, with no one coming to help her.

As you can probably imagine, that initial early childhood abuse made me pretty messed up. By the time I started school, I didn't really know how to respond in normal situations, and my behaviour could be pretty extreme. This meant I was being moved around a bit, and ended up going to three different primary schools.

At my first school I was having extreme reactions to small events, like those mentioned above. My responses to the abuse had stayed with me and I was extremely emotional. I also began lying to the other kids about my life to try to compensate for how different I felt. My responses and the lying made me an outcast from my peers, and they began bullying me pretty early on.

The first time I was moved to a new school because of this I was about seven, and I remember being really excited because it was a new start with new people. I was also really nervous, because I thought that starting a new school where everyone else already knew each other was going to be really difficult.

Only about a week into attending this school, I became the target of bullying from two of the 'popular girls', who began making fun of everything about me. My mum did try, but we were poor, so I never had the 'cool' clothes or the new toys. I often stole items of my uniform from the lost property bin, and found it so hard to fit in on mufti days.

I remember one day in particular, as it was one of those incidents that confirmed my negative beliefs about myself. It was interval, and I had run out to the junior playground with a bunch of kids from my class. I climbed up onto one of the wooden ledges and grabbed onto the monkey bars and started to swing across. I loved climbing and I loved the monkey bars, because I was pretty good at them.

When I landed at the other end of the bars, I heard snickering and then an outburst of laughter. I didn't really understand what was going on, but then one of the popular girls piped up and said, 'No one is going to touch those now, because no one wants to catch your disease.' My heart dropped into my stomach as I watched another kid try to wipe the bars I had just touched, while everyone else stood around and laughed. I jumped off the little wooden ledge and ran to the bathroom, where I sat and cried for the rest of interval. **Those words confirmed the beliefs I held that I was unwanted, that I didn't belong and that I was unlovable.**

What you have to understand is that while sitting here writing this story as a 24-year-old those words might not mean much, but to a seven-year-old they were everything. To me at that age, they confirmed the beliefs I held that I was unwanted, that I didn't belong and that I was unlovable. I had taken what these kids did and said as a factual statement about my identity, and my little brain had gone, 'If they say it and act like this then it must be true.'

The bullying continued throughout my primary-school years, with me never fitting in but always desperately wanting to. The teachers were aware of what was happening, but I would quickly gain a reputation as a 'nark' if I told anyone what was going on, so I stopped asking for help.

Over the next few years I began to lose my sense of who I was. I spent so much time trying to fit in, trying to be 'enough' for the kids at school. I would follow the crowds, losing the ability to form my own opinions because I feared backlash. Even if it was a simple stance on whether or not a T-shirt was cool, I would follow whatever the popular kid said. I took on everything that was said about me: that I was a loser, that I was unwanted, that no one could ever love me. I took these beliefs and I made them a part of who I was. These kids were part of reshaping the way I saw the world and the way I saw myself. **These kids were part of reshaping the way I saw the world and the way I saw myself.**

To try to avoid getting bullied as much as possible, I ended up being the teachers' pet, sticking close to them and at times literally spending lunchtimes walking around with them. I remember the sense of them caring when things went wrong.

What I took from that, as a seven-year-old girl, was that when things were hard, people cared. When I was getting bullied or kids were picking on me, the teachers in my world showed me what felt like love.

I wasn't used to being shown love like this. Looking back, I can see how seven-year-old me took this time of my life and allowed it to completely re-form the world that I lived in and my picture of myself in it. I can see how it reinforced my belief that I was never good enough, and the beginnings of me building so many masks and defence mechanisms to avoid being hurt. It's also why I started to believe that being in crisis meant I would receive love—even if only momentarily. It was this warped belief that would cause me enormous amounts of pain and difficulty when I was in my teenage years.

CHAPTER FIVE

Running away

For every person, the way their beliefs about themselves are expressed is different, and the ways that mine came out were very broken. My self-beliefs of 'I'm unlovable' and 'I'm a burden' become overwhelmingly obvious in my teenage years, after I moved to Auckland at the age of 16. They caused me to react and respond in ways that would destroy relationships and cause me to isolate myself. There would be a few people who I would allow into my struggles, but when I felt they were becoming too close or getting to know the 'real me' I would suddenly stop communicating with them and kick them out of my world.

Don't get me wrong—the majority of people in my life saw only this extremely happy and bubbly girl. But that was a mask, a mask of people-pleasing but also a way of ensuring that my friends didn't get close enough to hurt me.

I used to think that this mask was just me trying to hide, but once I started to look at my core beliefs, I also began to realise that my pretending to be happy and bubbly all the time was also a response to the thought that 'maybe people will like me if I act this way'. I so desperately wanted to feel accepted and loved that the mask I used to hide also became the mask I used to try to fit in. This response led to a broken pattern, because while I still held the self-belief of being unlovable it didn't matter how much I tried, I would always end up feeling like I was alone.

This mask also meant that in all of my friendships, I would never let anyone close enough to see the 'real me'. All my peers would see was this crazy-happy girl with nothing bad going on in her life. They would turn to me to help them solve their problems. I wanted them to think I was perfect.

I wasn't just having bad days—every single day, I was battling with wanting to die.

This obviously led to very one-way relationships that broke apart after a while. Even someone who I would have considered my best friend would eventually drift away.

When I was 16 years old, I went on a weekend trip to Auckland to visit a friend. It was my first time ever on a plane and I was so excited. As I landed in the city my heart started to flutter, and over the next few days I fell in love with Auckland. I had always wanted to be involved in the media industry, I think mainly because TV was an escape from reality for me, and Auckland was the place to do that. When I got home I couldn't stop thinking about Auckland and how much I wanted to get out of Timaru and move there.

At this time I was still attending school and also working at a local fish and chip shop in the weekends and at nights to earn money. I had started saving up to leave home when another huge bullying incident happened at school. A bunch of girls who had spread rumours about me started creating anonymous Bebo pages (what we had before Facebook, for those of you who are too young to know!) and used them to send me threats and hate messages. I couldn't handle it, so one day I started looking at flights to Auckland to just get away again for a while. There was a big music festival, Parachute, happening at the start of the year in a small town just out of Auckland, and so I decided that I wanted to go to that.

I thought that by moving to another city, all of my problems would disappear and my life would be great ... how wrong I was.

In January 2012, I booked a flight to Auckland and arranged a lift to the festival. But a couple of days after I had booked the trip the bullying got even worse. I just wanted to die. I remember sitting in my room thinking, 'I can't go back to school this year. I can't stay in this town. If I do, I am going to kill myself.'

So, I walked out into the living room and told my mum that I was going to cancel my return flight and that I wanted to move to Auckland permanently. To be honest, I don't actually remember how this went down with her, but she did agree to let me go. I was determined to be independent and to try to escape the hell I was living in.

I packed my bags—two suitcases, to be exact—and got on a plane. I didn't really know anyone in Auckland but that didn't bother me—I was just excited that I was moving away from my childhood memories, the high-school bullying and the anxiety of feeling like the whole town hated me. I thought that by moving to another city, all of my problems would disappear and my life would be great...

Oh, how wrong I was. I very quickly discovered that I could run away from my situation, but I couldn't run away from myself.

*

When I moved to Auckland and started at a new high school, I tried to create an entirely new identity for myself. I didn't want to be seen the same way I had been in Timaru, and so despite the fact I was feeling nervous and terrible inside, I put a smile on my face and went to school every day being the 'nice new girl'. It wasn't long before the popular kids were hanging out with me—something that had never happened before. Maybe this time things were going to be different!

School in Auckland seemed pretty different to Timaru. For starters, the uniform rules were totally opposite—in Timaru we had a strict dress code and our hair always had to be tied up. They were pretty chill at my new school. It was also the first time that I had gone to a co-ed high school, so that was pretty weird for me to adjust to.

Not long after I moved to Auckland, I drank alcohol for the first time. It was my birthday and the other kids wanted to throw a party for me, so I went along with it. I was never into drinking or partying. I hated the taste of alcohol and I also associated the party scene with 'popular mean girls', because that was who seemed to do the partying. But now I was in a new city, I pretended to be really into it and acted like I did this kind of thing all the time.

None of the kids here knew that back home I was one of the most hated kids in school. They all liked the person I was pretending to be, and not the real me. Inside though, I did not want to be there. I felt so out of place and uncomfortable.

But the real me showed her face after another party, where I ended up on the couch with some guy from my year level. He was a classic school jock and he was lying up against me while another friend was asleep on the other couch. We were underneath a blanket because it was cold, just lying there. Then I felt his breathing begin to quicken and suddenly I felt his hand on me. I froze. I didn't know what to say or do, so I just stayed where I was. He then whispered to me, 'Let's go into the bedroom.'

There was no way I could go through with that. I was so scared, and all the memories from my childhood came to the forefront of my mind. I kicked him out of the house, but then my built-up identity as the 'cool girl' was shattered and everyone was talking about me. I was never the 'party animal' I pretended to be—I was just trying to fit in. That mask had failed me and left me worse off.

*

My home life in Auckland quickly turned into a disaster, too. At first I started out living with a family with young children, and I desperately wanted them to like me. The mum had been great, helping me enrol into the local high school and giving me super-cheap rent since I couldn't afford much.

While things seemed to be going OK for a while, it wasn't long before the warped beliefs I held started to ramp up and I tried to hurt myself. When I woke up in hospital the next day, I found out that the family I had been living with had decided that it wasn't a good idea for me to go back to their house because of their young children.

As the nurse explained this to me, I burst into tears. I must have really disturbed the rest of the people in my shared hospital room, because I was so upset I was hyperventilating. I was so scared and broken. I didn't have anywhere to go—I had only just moved to Auckland and I still didn't really know anyone that well. I was stranded.

One of the people I had become friends with at school came to visit me in the hospital (not knowing why I was actually there). She said she knew some people I could move in with. And that's how I came to be living with the people doing drugs and robberies.

I so desperately wanted to feel accepted and loved that the mask I used to hide also became the mask I used to try to fit in.

After the police raid, I got moved into emergency accommodation and then into a women's refuge. Then, one of the police officers working on the case decided to take me in, to live with her and her family. She got me into a new school, which was great, but I soon fell into my old patterns of trying so hard to be accepted and not knowing how to respond under stress. After only about four months my behaviours ramped up again and I was in and out of hospital several times, following self-harm and suicide attempts.

Funnily enough, though, while my situation was pretty horrible, I still felt I had made the right decision in leaving Timaru. I know that may seem pretty crazy, but the reality was that Timaru held such horrible memories and people, and at least in Auckland I had the opportunity to try to make something a little different for myself. I also liked it because for a while nobody knew me. While I kept changing schools and houses it meant that I could 'start over' again and again, and hope that I could make friends this time around.

Then things got much worse. One day I was on the school bus and a few girls from my old school in Auckland were on it. My heart started pounding when I saw them, and as I went to get off, one of them came up to me and punched me in the face. She told me to watch my back because they were after me.

I had been in Auckland for only nine months at this stage, and I had already been to two different schools and lived in five different houses. I had changed the town I lived in, but the prison of my mind had come with me. There is nothing like being homeless to reinforce your feelings of being alone, unlovable and unwanted.

*

Within that first year in Auckland I tried to take my life three times. Unlike when I was 12 and was being bullied at school, this time I couldn't pin it on something that had happened to me, because this time the circumstances were self-made. The reality was that I was living in a way that made me hate myself so much, and if I hated me, then how could anyone love me?

I began living in a constant crisis state, believing that people would only care about me if there were things going on. And by constant crisis state, I don't mean I was just having bad days—I meant that every single day, I was battling with wanting to die. Every week there would be some kind of crisis or drama in my life, often self-made.

After a while I became unable to live without being in this constant state of crisis, because being in that state meant people cared about me. It might only be short-term, but it was the only way I would feel the tiniest bit loved.

However, the thing is, the way that I was acting was really too much for anyone to handle. The people in my life were getting phone calls every few weeks to say that I was in hospital again, getting goodbye notes or seeing me hurt myself.

Because I was acting like this, my belief that I was a burden to other people really began to rear its head. I felt like I was wasting everyone's time, and that they would be happier without me here. I was a prisoner in my own mind and I couldn't find an escape. I would be stuck on repeat in this awful cycle that would say 'I have to act this way for people to love me', followed by 'No one could ever love me anyway', then around to 'Because of the way I have acted, I am a burden to everyone and I don't deserve to be alive.'

This was the pattern of my life from when I was 16 till I was 20. I could not tell you how many nights I spent in hospital or how often I would sit in my room or the bathroom crying, just wishing that I could be someone else.

That I could be someone that people actually loved and wanted to be around.

CHAPTER SIX

Downward spiral

In 2013, while I was studying acting at Excel School of Performing Arts in Auckland, a group of the other students started to attend Equippers Church on a Sunday. I decided to join them one week and I absolutely loved it, so kept going. Faith became a very big part of my journey, giving me something bigger than myself to hold onto and making me feel like there was a bigger purpose in life. For someone who was very good at isolating, having an entire church and community of people who chose to love me through all of my difficulties was huge.

The following year, I decided to study leadership at Equippers College, which is part of the Equippers Church. At the start of the year I met the two people who founded the creative side of the college, Wayne and Libby. Wayne and Libby are pastors in the church, the founders of the creative stream of the college I was attending, and are also the parents of my friend Grace.

I actually remember to this day the exact moment that Grace and I met. We had both attended a creative night at Equippers Church in 2013, and were standing outside the theatre at the end of the night. I had already met Wayne and Libby in passing at church by this stage, and so Libby came up to us and introduced us. Right at that moment, fireworks went off above the theatre, and we stood there making jokes about it being a sign that we would be good friends.

Grace and I started to hang out, bonding over our love of crazy adventures (I took her sky-diving for her twenty-first birthday!), good food and strong coffee. She is such a fun person to be around—one of those friends who can make you laugh in the midst of your darkest days.

After I enrolled in Equippers College I began to see Wayne and Libby most days in class. At this time I was in the middle of some pretty rough stuff, and with them both being in leadership roles and me being familiar with them through Grace, I was naturally drawn to them. Six years later, Grace, her brother Josh and her parents Wayne and Libby have become my family. However, it took one heck of a journey to get to that point. For the next two years I pushed these relationships to the limits.

There was another person who I became close to over this time, too. Esther, who I mentioned in chapter 1, was also involved with Equippers, and became part of my support network.

I have known her for many years, from even before I moved up to Auckland. As I said earlier I met Esther for the first time when I was 12 years old, and I saw her as part of an anti-bullying schools roadshow called the Revolution Tour. I was having a hard time in life at that point, and as I sat there and listened to her speak, something inside of me felt like she understood my struggles. I ended up going up to her after the show and talking to her. She encouraged me, told me that I had a great future ahead of me and reminded me that hope was real.

After we had talked that night, I added her as a Facebook friend, and then, thanks to the power of social media, we had kept in touch, messaging every so often. Once I moved up to Auckland and started attending Equippers Church, it turned out that Esther went there too. Although it had been four years since Esther had come to my school and our communication on social media had faded as life moved on, once I started going to Equippers we started talking again. We quickly became close, especially once I started going to Equippers College, where she was teaching communication. Along with Wayne and Libby, she also saw me at my worst fairly early on. She saw me break down, repeatedly end up in hospital, stuck in a suicidal pattern, all while trying to pretend to others that everything was OK.

At the moment Grace and I met, fireworks went off above the theatre. We stood there making jokes about it being a sign that we would be good friends.

For the whole of that year I was attending Equippers College I was fighting an intense internal battle—discovering people actually cared about me, but also not knowing if I wanted them to. In my mind, if people cared for me and I let them in, then there was a high chance they would leave me. (I didn't understand why that was at this time, but it was something I would soon discover, which I'll share with you soon.)

I spent a lot of 2014 running out of classes at college because of different things that would come up and trigger my emotions. Twice, this led to me trying to take my life, and other times it led to me pushing Libby and Wayne and Esther away, because I was so sure they would abandon me soon anyway.

However, while one part of me was living in a crisis mode, part of me was also really enjoying the year. I was making new friends, I was involved in this amazing church and I was learning new things every day. I started to get involved in the kids' programme through the practical side of the college, which I also loved.

From the outside this may seem confusing—how could I be both a normal and happy teenager, and yet still be suicidal? If you've been there, you can understand it. Many people who are struggling with mental health also have the ability to get involved in things, make friends and have a good time. But there is always this little voice in your mind that will say 'you are not good enough' or 'they don't actually like you'. So while I was surrounded by the most incredible people, the negative side of my mind took over at times.

I remember one day in particular when I had got upset and run out of class. Although I can't remember why, I got hold of a suicide method. I sat in a park and began the process of trying to take my life. I then sat on a bench in the drizzling rain, reading back text messages Esther had previously sent me—messages where she told me she believed in me and that she loved me.

Those messages were enough to stop me in my tracks and make me go back to the college. It took a lot of courage to walk back up to the office and face up to the consequences of the stupid decision I had just made. The staff there called the mental-health crisis team and they said I needed to go down to the hospital to be checked, because of what I had done. I was so mad—I thought I would be fine, but they still had to clear me. I was mortified, I felt terrible and thoughts that I was a being a burden to those around me overcame my mind.

Esther took me down to the hospital and sat with me for a while, then as she left, Libby came in. At that time, I couldn't understand why they were spending so much of their time with me. To be honest, my mind told me it was because they had to take an interest in the wellbeing of their students as part of their work at the college. Looking back now, I can see that while, yes, part of it was them doing their jobs, they were also there because they genuinely cared about me. However, at that time my mental state wouldn't let me believe that. **How could I be both a normal and happy teenager, and yet still be suicidal? Many people who are struggling with mental health also**

have the ability to get involved in things, but there is always this little voice in your mind that will say 'you are not good enough'.

As Libby was sitting there, a nurse came in and asked me to fill out a form with all of my details. On the form I had to put down two 'next of kin' contacts, but I didn't know what to write down. Libby saw me staring at the form, so she grabbed it from my hands and put herself down. I felt guilty, thinking that she had felt she had to do that; however, I now know that she did it because she cared for me and wanted to help me.

As I sat on the bed, she sat on a chair beside me, telling me that I was more loved than I knew and that I didn't need to do stuff like this. Hearing her say that was comforting, but once again caused my mind to twist it back into 'She is just saying that because she has to.' (Again, with the benefit of rational hindsight, not true!) About six hours later I got medically cleared and Libby was the one who took me home.

CHAPTER SEVEN

Crisis

I continued to live in this constant state of crisis all year, putting up a million walls every day. I also tried to take my life again a few months later. When things got too much and I couldn't control my emotions I would end up running away, either from class, or from events or meetings. I didn't know how to articulate my feelings or tell people that I needed help or that I was starting to feel down—the only way I could 'deal' with it was by running.

I would lie to people, saying that one thing was going on when it was actually something else. This was a protective mechanism I used to try to still get the help I needed without people having to know the reality of what was actually going on in my mind and in my life. I was embarrassed that I couldn't control my emotions, and I was afraid that if people knew what was really going on then they would hate me.

Surprisingly, through all of this I was still pretty high-functioning. I was able to put on my mask of 'being OK' and attend classes most days, study and socialise with people. In fact, a lot of my friends would have had no idea what was going on. I could be happy and talkative during the day, and then as soon as I was alone at home I would crash down. I was so afraid of being on my own because that meant my mind was free to wander ... and that is exactly what it did.

A lot of people would see my behaviour during this time as attention-seeking (see chapter 18), but I now know it was my core beliefs of being unlovable and a burden ramping up. I was acting out of brokenness, testing relationships to see when they would fail, because I believed that everyone I loved or who loved me would eventually leave.

I was spinning a web and living in a false sense of reality ... so much so that I found myself in the same situation as when I was a kid, not knowing who I really was. To be honest, I'm not sure I ever really knew who I was. I was so busy pretending everything was OK and trying to fit in with my peers, but also generating drama so that I could have a sense of feeling loved by those in 'mentor'-type roles.

Cutting myself off allowed me to go back to my old behaviours of self-harming, trying to take my life and lying to people.

It was almost like I was living a split life. Different groups of people saw different sides of me, but nobody ever saw the 'real' me—both because I didn't know who the real me was and also because I feared them knowing what I was really like. I would spend night after night looking in the mirror with tears rolling down my cheeks, hating what looked back at me. Hating the girl I had become—the kind of girl who had no real friendships because she put a mask on with everybody and pretended to be someone she wasn't. The kind of girl who would have extreme reactions to the smallest things and lived in constant fear of abandonment. The kind of girl who believed that nobody could ever love her, and that the world would be better without her. The girl who would be in hospital every couple of months, or would be found on the edge of a cliff wanting to jump. The girl who would lie, hide and assume everyone hated her. I never understood this girl and for years I hated her with everything in me.

*

In 2015 I experienced what was probably one of the hardest years of my life. It was the year that a young girl who I had been trying to help took her life, and also the year that I chose to try to walk away from the people who actually cared about me. I stopped going to the church and I began to spiral downwards in a way that I never had before.

Every single day my head was filled with coming up with a plan to take my life. I would walk around with a suicide method in my bag at all times, just waiting for the perfect time. It was a dangerous security blanket for me—ironically one that reduced rather than increased my safety. Esther kept messaging me but I had stopped engaging because in my mind, she, Wayne and Libby had got to know me too well. They knew all of my flaws, all of the broken parts, and I was sure that it was only a matter of time before they left, so I thought I had to leave first.

Cutting myself off from them also allowed me to go back to my old behaviours of self-harming, trying to take my life and lying to people, trying to be someone I wasn't—pretending to be that happy-go-lucky girl who had it all together and was succeeding in life. I was so torn. A big part of me just wanted to run back to the people who knew me and get help, but I was also too ashamed to reach out.

It got to the point where I made one of the stupidest decisions of my life. I tried to run away to Australia, to do the same thing I had when I left Timaru for Auckland a few years earlier. It was a very spontaneous decision, where I had the thought and then booked a one-way flight that same day.

I remember seeing Wayne briefly in the church foyer just before I left—I had come back to church for the first time in a while and I bumped into him as I was walking out. He said, 'Jazz, I think you are running away ... If you go over there and it doesn't work after six months, then please just come home.' I turned to him and said, 'I know exactly what I'm doing. I'm not running.'

Spoiler alert ... I was running. It lasted all of about three weeks. I got over to Melbourne and was staying with a friend of mine I had met at an event a few years earlier. I had plans to go to an acting school there, but never actually finished the application. I didn't know anyone there except my one friend I was staying with, but I actually liked that. I wanted to start again where no one knew me, in the hope that I could create a new reality. Of course, that didn't work (which I should have learnt when I first moved to Auckland).

Despite not being a drinker, when I was staying with this friend we went out one night and I drank a lot. So much that I don't remember the majority of the night, but I woke up with a guy in my bed the next morning. I didn't remember anything—not how he got there or what we had done. I had never even willingly kissed a guy before that because I was so scared following my childhood experiences, so waking up to this was a shock.

I remember kicking him out of my friend's house and then sitting on my bed crying. I had never done something like that before—I had got drunk just because I wanted to fit in with my friend and I didn't like it at all.

I messaged Esther and Libby, telling them what had happened and how upset I was. Both of them replied, saying how sorry they were that I had done that. They encouraged me to go and shower and try to go to church (it was a Sunday morning).

At this point I already knew that I had really screwed up. I just wanted to go home but I was too scared. Everyone knew I had moved to Australia and I felt like if I went home then people would all be talking about me and how I failed.

However, later that afternoon, a friend of mine from Equippers, Georgia, started messaging me on Snapchat. She was just asking me how Australia was going and I didn't tell her what had happened, but she picked up that something seemed off with me. She then messaged, 'You do know that it is OK to go back home, right? No one is going to be talking about it, or thinking you failed. If home is the best place for you, then you need to do what is best for you.'

I didn't really know Georgia that well, but her words really stuck with me and I ended up booking a flight home later that week, arriving back in Auckland even more broken than I had been when I left.

*

Once I got back, I had my worst ever bout of suicidal thoughts and attempts. My belief that I was a burden was throwing me into a strong determination to die and so I tried to take my life, several times. I knew I needed help, but I didn't know how to ask for it. I just self-destructed.

I was running out of my house to go and hurt myself in random parks and forests. The police were smashing windows to get into my house while I was sitting there trying to take my life. There were nights when they would literally have to chase me down the street and handcuff me for my own protection.

During this period of my life, everything seemed to escalate as I spiralled out of control. I remember being filled with so much fear that I couldn't sleep.

In early 2015, someone tried to break into my house one night when I was there alone and from that moment onwards I was filled with crippling fear that created some pretty intense behaviours. I quickly became unable to settle at night, I would have full blown panic attacks and, eventually, I began sleeping with a knife beside my bed. Even though logically it wasn't wise, it made me feel somewhat safe for a while. However, it wasn't long until my anxiety picked up again and I began to spiral so far out of control that I would leave my house and just walk around the street until about 3a.m. with the knife in my pocket for protection. I didn't feel safe in my own house and my mind had gripped onto this belief that the only way I could control my anxiety and feel a bit secure was to walk around and see the world still kind of moving.

I wholeheartedly believed that the world would be better off without me in it. I tried to commit suicide *eight times* that year, and became so well known to the police that I was labelled a 'red alert', meaning that if there was a call made about me I was first priority because I was at such a high risk.

One time I had run up to the edge of a cliff and sat there for about half an hour, thinking whether this was how I wanted to die. Just as I decided that this was it and went to jump, I felt arms wrap around me. The next couple of minutes were filled with me trying to fight off police officers and jump off the cliff. My hospital files say 'The police have brought Jazz into ED, all of them are clearly covered in mud and police say that they had to really battle to get her off the edge.'

That suicide attempt led to me getting admitted into the psych ward. It was the first time I had ever been admitted to the ward before, and I don't think anything could have prepared me for what was about to happen.

CHAPTER EIGHT

Psych ward

I had spent the majority of the night in the Emergency Department, and at about 1.30a.m. the psychiatric liaison person walked into the room and told me they were going to admit me into the mental-health ward. Everything inside of me felt sick—I had tried to take my life before, many times, but this was the first time that they had actually put me into the ward. The psych ward was in the hospital grounds, but in a separate building to the main hospital.

Half an hour later she came back into my room and said, 'OK, get up, we are moving you now. There is a car outside and I am going to sit in the back with you. You're not going to try to run, are you? Do we need security?' I was done fighting them at this stage—I was exhausted and tired, so I assured them I wouldn't run, and we walked out and sat in the car. It was dark and freezing cold as we drove over to the psych ward.

Because it was the early hours of the morning, the main reception wasn't open, meaning that we had to go around to the back entrance. This made the whole experience so much worse. The psych liaison walked me to the waiting area, down a corridor that was long, dirty and off-white. I sat down on a couch and watched my escort leave the room with one of the nurses from the ward.

She was doing her best to help me feel like I wasn't a lost cause—that it was possible to laugh again and think and talk about things that were not suicide.

About five minutes later they walked back in and told me to stand up. The nurse introduced herself as Rebecca and did my obs, checking blood pressure, temperature, etc. Then she began to look at me up and down.

At first I didn't know what she was doing, but then she said 'I'm sorry, but I need you to take off your hoodie string and your shoe laces.' In hindsight that made sense, but at the time I remember my heart started to beat faster as I began to slowly but surely lose the control that I had once held so tightly. The minimal belongings I had on me were put in a little plastic bag with a hospital sticker with my name placed on it. The psych liaison said her goodbyes, telling me that she hoped I could 'sort this out', and then I was left in the care of Rebecca.

As the door closed behind the liaison, the reality of my situation and where I was suddenly hit me, and I burst into tears. I was so scared—I did not want to be there, I was supposed to die but now I was locked in this ward.

We started walking down another dark and cold corridor towards the Intensive Care part of the ward and I began to resist a little bit, afraid of what I was about to walk into. Rebecca gently took my arm, reassuring me that it was going to be OK, and we walked through to what would become my room. It had a big, heavy, white door with a glass window cut into it so that the nurses could make sure I was safe at all times. The floor was cold, grey, polished concrete, and the bed sat in the corner of the room with nothing but a white sheet and thin white blanket on top of it. There was a brown wooden desk against one of the other walls, next to a matching brown closet. The room was stripped of anything you could possibly ever hurt yourself with. **As the door closed, the reality of my situation suddenly hit me, and I burst into tears. I was so scared—I was supposed to die but now I was locked in this ward.**

I walked over and sat on the bed, leaning against the wall with my knees curled up to my chest. I continued to cry. Rebecca came and sat next to me, putting her hand on my shoulder to try to console me. Her shift was supposed to have ended an hour earlier but she was still there because of my admission, so it wasn't long before she had to give me medication to put me to sleep and leave for the night.

The medication did its job pretty fast, but it wasn't long before I woke up to the sound of a middle-aged man screaming. I got up and looked outside the window in my door and saw nurses trying to tackle a naked man. For a girl who has been sexually abused, seeing this set me off into a quick spiral. I started having a panic attack, shaking and crying to the point that I eventually had to press the call bell in my room and a new nurse came in. She gave me more medication to calm me down, and then sat with me for about half an hour. We talked about what had happened the night before and why I felt like this and she began asking me the questions I came to know too well: 'On a scale of one to ten, how is your mood?' 'On a scale of one to ten, how strong are the feelings of wanting to take your life?' My mood was a one and my urges about an eight at that stage!

The next few days in the Intensive Care part of the ward were rough. I refused to leave my room, and I looked forward only to when Rebecca would come back on as my nurse. Rebecca had something about her that made me feel just a little less crazy. She would tell me about what she was doing in the gym, her kids and her partner. She would tell me her dreams and ask me about mine. Rebecca was doing her best to help me feel like I wasn't a lost cause and that it was possible to laugh again and think and talk about things that were not suicide.

Four days later I was moved into the open part of the ward, which was a lot nicer than Intensive Care. There were two open wards, Ward A and Ward B, connected by a corridor. Off this were meeting rooms and a large occupational therapy area, filled with art supplies, gym equipment, massage chairs and puzzles. It wasn't good-quality stuff, but it was something. Each ward also had a large lounge area with a table tennis table in the middle and lots of couches spread around. There was a TV room (that I never set foot in) and a kitchen, and after a few days I started to come out of my room and into these common areas. While I was in the open ward I also started to receive counselling, seeing a psychologist every few days and doing some occupational therapy like painting, drawing and even playing table tennis.

My weeks spent in this ward were rocky. There were times when I felt pretty good, and others when I tried to escape from the hospital or find things to cut myself with. Once one of the nurses walked in to find I had turned my entire room upside down and I had cut all over my body. She cleaned everything up and bandaged me as I just sat crying, then she gave me medication that helped calm me down and continued to sit with me until the wave had passed.

I continued to have these waves of intense behaviour, trying to hurt myself, so eventually I got readmitted to the Intensive Care unit of the mental-health ward. While I was in there, Wayne and Libby came in to see me. I sat on the couch in an interview room dressed in baggy clothes and filled with drugs to keep me somewhat calm. I remember looking at them and just bursting into tears. I felt so guilty seeing them there, knowing they knew everything I had done, and yet when I looked at them I also saw peace, kindness and the kind of love that doesn't give up.

I looked at the other people in the ward who were way older than me and still fighting, and thought, 'If I don't do something soon, I am either going to be sixty and still in this ward, or dead.'

They spoke hope to me, saying that this wasn't the kind of life I had to live. They told me that they knew and understood that I was seriously struggling, but that there was still hope for change. They told me there was still a chance for me to make it through this and come out the other side.

During that conversation I had the tiniest piece of willpower restored to me. I was at my absolute worst, and they were still there, choosing to love me.

I had been looking at the other people in the ward who were way older than me and still fighting, and I remember thinking, 'If I don't do something soon, I am either going to be sixty and still in this ward, or dead.'

I knew that I had to beat this somehow, but I didn't know where to start. At this stage I hadn't figured out how to fight, and it wasn't until my final suicide attempt, a couple of months and another admission later, and that conversation with Esther that I really decided to fight through this and figure out where my destructive beliefs had even come from. Looking back, there had been many moments when people had spoken of hope to me and gone out of their way to help me. I couldn't see it at the time, but those moments kept me going. But it wasn't until that final suicide attempt that it became clear to me why I was still going around in the same cycle, and decided to get out of it.

CHAPTER NINE

Breaking the beliefs

In order to combat this destructive thinking that had kept me in this cycle for years, I decided to get practical. I realised that just recognising my core beliefs and talking about wanting to change them without actually *doing* anything to change them wasn't going to get me out of the cycle I had been in for years. I needed to take action.

Two main beliefs I wanted to change were 'I am a burden' and 'I am unlovable', because I knew that they were the biggest contributors to my warped sense of identity and self-worth. I wrote those two core beliefs on one side of a piece of paper and drew a line down the middle of the page. Then, over the next few months I would write down everything that those closest to me would say or do that *contradicted* those beliefs—things like 'Jazz, I love you' or 'Jazz, I'm proud of you'. I wrote down the things people had done that proved my beliefs wrong. I wrote down that Wayne and Libby had come to visit me in the mental-health ward—even the simple fact that Wayne, Esther and Libby were still standing alongside me despite my many, many mess-ups.

This list wasn't something that anyone told me to do—it was my own idea. (I was seeing a counsellor but at this stage wasn't really engaging with them—more on that later.) But it meant that every time my mind would say 'Jazz, you're a burden' or 'You're unlovable', I could pull out this list and confront myself with rock-hard evidence that my internal reality—what my mind was saying—didn't match the external truth. The truth that I was loved, that I wasn't a burden.

My list of core beliefs and the evidence that contradicted them became a vital part in my recovery. I recorded every word that people around me said, every action that backed up those words. There were many people that contributed to this list without knowing, and to be honest, some of them probably still don't know that their words played a part in breaking those beliefs that would send me into a downward spiral almost every week. **Even once my major mental-health crisis was over, my thoughts and beliefs were something I still continued to struggle with and had to work for a long time to overcome.**

Everyone has their own set of core beliefs about themselves. Even if it is not you who is struggling with these beliefs, chances are some of the people around you are.

Remember, your words can hold the power of life or death. Everything you say matters. At the beginning of this section

I talked about how words have the ability to contribute to negative beliefs that can form your identity, but they also have the ability to turn someone's life around. For me, words played a huge part in forming the negative beliefs in my life, and so words also played a huge part in undoing them and creating new ones.

Your words have the ability to be part of changing someone's world, for worse or for better—use them wisely.

*

Even once my major mental-health crisis was over, my thoughts and beliefs were something I continued to struggle with and had to work for a long time to overcome. I would still get attacks of these overwhelming emotions and feel like a burden, but after I had managed to stop myself responding to them by trying to kill myself, I didn't actually know how to deal with them. I no longer wanted to take my life, but that coping response was all I had known for years.

Everyone has their own set of core beliefs about themselves. Even if it is not you who is struggling with these beliefs, chances are some of the people around you are.

Another one of my coping mechanisms was to bury myself in work, as this was something I had done since I was a kid. I remember my teachers at school always saying I was going to burn out because of how much I got involved in. I had a really high capacity for work, and while I do love being involved in lots of things, it became my new coping mechanism. This meant that even once I was in a better place mentally, I kept myself busy all the time. I took pride in people saying, 'Wow, Jazz, you are so busy' because my beliefs would still tell me that I, as a person, wasn't enough, and that I had to be constantly achieving things to be noticed and valued.

This was something I struggled with until pretty recently, to be honest. Even among all of my Voices of Hope work, speaking, writing and touring, I still at times fell back into my default position of being 'too busy'. The reality was that I *was* busy, juggling what felt like a million things at once, but the people closest to me could tell I was getting overwhelmed and emotional, which raised a red flag.

I remember one time in about mid-2018, walking up to the church car park with Wayne and Libby. As we got to my car I looked up to say goodbye. They knew that I wasn't feeling OK (they both know me so well they can see straight through me now!), so they started asking questions about why I seemed down.

I had had a really difficult week: I was overwhelmed by the number of suicidal young girls I was communicating with, and I had been given four people's suicide methods, which were in my car. As I was talking about how exhausted I was and how I was really struggling, Wayne and Libby turned and me and said, 'Jazz, remember that we love you for who you are, not what you do.' Those words hit me like a ton of bricks. I burst into tears, as if a huge weight had been lifted.

While I was no longer suicidal at this point, I still had a belief that people only loved me for what I did. But that wasn't the case, and it took time and constantly reminding myself of the truth for me to slowly start to realise it was true. I went back to the strategy I had used for my other core beliefs and used it again to help break this one. And that helped me to learn that I could drop everything I was doing and it wouldn't matter, because I would still be loved and accepted for who I was.

I recently read a quote from neuroscientist Dr Caroline Leaf that says, 'We need to stop glorifying the person who "works all weekend" and rather praise the person who succeeds in finding a balance between work, family and rest. Our culture of celebrating the workaholic is one of the main reasons we are seeing an increase in mental, emotional and physical burnout.' I couldn't agree more!

CHAPTER TEN

Speaking hope

There were many moments in the months and years after my last suicide attempt that helped to chip away at my negative core beliefs, but it took a long time to begin to create new thought patterns and beliefs. It was up to me to choose to believe those closest to me when they said they loved me, rather than telling myself that they were 'just saying that'.

One of the biggest examples of something that helped me to unpick those old beliefs happened on 21 June, 2015. Every aspect of that night is ingrained in my brain—for many reasons, the main one being that it was a night that really shifted my perspective.

I was attending a church conference with my flatmate and some friends. We were all driving into the conference sessions together over several days.

This particular day I had woken up feeling really horrible. I don't think anything specific triggered those feelings, but I decided to stay home and not go to the conference sessions that day. Instead, I sat at home, dwelling on my emotions, listening to sad music and thinking back on every reason that I should be dead.

It took a long time to begin to create new thought patterns and beliefs. It was up to me to choose to believe those closest to me when they said they loved me.

To anyone who hasn't experienced mental-health problems, this might be confusing. How do you go from being fine one day to not wanting to live the next? The human brain is complex, and, unfortunately, this is the reality for some people living with mental illness.

As the afternoon rolled around I decided that I needed to try to pull myself out of this state, so I caught the bus down to the stadium where the conference was being held. I walked into the arena and felt my chest tightening as I was swallowed by the crowd. I looked around at the hundreds of people standing in the foyer, and in that moment I felt more alone than ever. There is nothing more isolating than being in a room full of people and realising that no one knows that just a few hours ago you were contemplating taking your life.

I managed to get myself into the main arena and sit through the evening session, then I found my flatmate and a friend and we got in the car to come home.

The entire drive home my thoughts were running a million miles an hour, and by the time we got there I had decided that I just needed to do it, once and for all. I needed to end everything, because everyone would be better off without me.

When we got home, my friend and my flatmate went to the living room and I went down the hallway to my bedroom. I grabbed a pen and paper and wrote a suicide note and jumped out my window to the back yard. I didn't want anyone to realise where I was going or to try to stop me. By this point it was about 10p.m. and it was absolutely freezing.

I ran down towards the local park, grabbed my phone out of my pocket and then texted Esther goodbye. As I began the process of trying to take my life, I remembered what had happened with that young girl I had been trying to help, who had disappeared after she had sent out goodbye messages. I remembered how sick I felt every minute that she was missing, before she had been found dead.

There is nothing more isolating than being in a room full of people and realising that no one knows that just a few hours ago you were contemplating taking your life.

So I made a decision that I now realise actually saved my life that night. I called the police and said, 'I'm sorry, but I am going to kill myself and I don't want to be missing for ages or for some poor member of the public to find my body.' I then told them my location and hung up.

As I began the process of taking my life I suddenly heard a door slam somewhere above me. The area I was in backed onto a row of houses, and as I glanced up I saw a woman standing on her balcony. I was stuck in that moment, so afraid that she would see me, because the last thing I wanted was to ruin another person's life by having them find my dead body. So I stood in silence and waited for her to go back inside. A few minutes later she turned around, went inside and turned off the porch light.

As I turned back around I saw flashlights in the far corner of the park and I knew that I needed to act now. As I went to jump, however, my jacket got caught on a branch. The sound of my jacket ripping alerted the police officers, who were directly below me. I felt hands suddenly grip my back, and for the next five minutes I fought the two police officers as they tried to get to me. I remember kicking and screaming and feeling so distraught that my plan had been ruined. I knew the process I was about to go through: being taken by the police to the Emergency Department ... sitting in the psych room for six hours with police guarding the door ... the assessments, the questions ... and then either getting told 'you'll be fine' and let go, or being stuck in a psych ward. I was terrified. I just wanted to be dead.

The police officers took me to their car and put me in the back, where the female constable sat with me and held me. I sat there curled up in a ball, crying my heart out, as this amazing woman, Constable Meika Campbell, tried to console me, talking to me about hope and trying to get me to open up as to why I had tried to end my life.

Eventually I got up the courage to look up at her, and I saw tears rolling down her cheeks too. I was confused. Why was she crying? Why did she care?

We stayed in the back of the police car until the ambulance arrived, and then she got in the back of it with me and came down to the hospital. I was crying the whole way, just wanting them to let me go. We arrived at the hospital and I got taken to the psych room, and the familiar process began.

However, this time Constable Campbell decided to sit on my bed with me, talking with me until way past her shift ended. For the rest of the night she stayed by my side and talked to me about this thing called 'hope'. When she eventually had to go, she said to me, 'I want you to text me tomorrow and tell me you are OK. I believe in you. You can do this.

For the rest of the night she stayed by my side and talked to me about this thing called 'hope'. She said to me, 'I believe in you. You can do this.'

'You need to make it to your twenty-first birthday. If you can do that for me, I will come and find you on that day to say happy birthday.'

For some time after this night she messaged me, encouraging me and speaking hope to me alongside the important people in my life.

About a year after this attempt I hit my twenty-first birthday. By this stage, I had forgotten her promise—but she hadn't. She came to my house and knocked on my door just to wish me a happy birthday, and to celebrate the fact that I was still alive and fighting. Constable Campbell is another person who taught me that maybe, just maybe,

I wasn't unlovable, and maybe I was worth fighting for.

*

Fast-forward three years and things had changed drastically in my life, for the better (we will get to that later on!). I decided to write an open letter to Constable Campbell, thanking her for what she had done that night, on my charity page Voices of Hope. We had stayed in touch over the years, chatting online from time to time, but I hadn't actually seen her since my twenty-first birthday.

I had been scrolling through Facebook and seeing a whole bunch of articles slamming the police, talking about how horrible they were. I wanted to show the public that this wasn't true, and in a way try to instil hope and trust in our police force. So I wrote the letter, recalling the events of the night in 2015 when Constable Campbell and her partner had come to my aid. I ended the letter like this:

You went over and beyond your 'job requirements'. I often see police being slammed in the media for all kinds of things, but the public don't often see this side — the people, stories and emotions behind our police force. Thank you, Constable Campbell, for not only physically saving my life that night, but for speaking hope, for sitting with me, crying with me and seeing a future for me that at that point I couldn't see. A future I am now living in.

Everything I now get to do, every video I create, talk I give or mental-health campaign I organise would not have happened had you not stepped in that night. Your intervention and care ensured that I lived to see breakthrough and freedom.

Thank you for putting your life on the line for our country and, while doing so, saving mine.

I uploaded the letter onto Facebook and what happened next I could never have never imagined. It absolutely blew up, going viral. It was covered by media all over the world and I was flooded with messages from the public—and from police—thanking me for writing the letter. Constable Campbell also messaged me on Facebook saying how amazing the letter was and how she felt honoured to be part of my journey.

That night with Constable Campbell was one of my significant turning points, but I still had to work through the process of confronting and dismantling my core beliefs, which had been built up over years. There is no doubt, though, this incident gave me yet another shove in the right direction.

Section Two

FEARS

CHAPTER ELEVEN

Abandonment

Abandoned: Being deserted or left.

When we are adults, the different actions and behaviours we display in relationships are often influenced by fears and beliefs about things that happened when we were children. For some, it might be a significant event like abuse, the death of someone close, or a parent leaving. For others it may have been observing a parent who had multiple partners, moving cities or moving schools. The event doesn't have to be huge, and it also may not have seemed significant at the time to the child, but the effects on the child's developing brain and thought patterns can be huge.

The fear of being abandoned is one of the most common psychological fears, and it was certainly a huge one for me. Rooted in childhood, this fear can grow to paralyse people emotionally and prevent them from forming healthy, strong relationships, whether they are romantic relationships or friendships. This fear can also lead to impulsive behaviour, risky relationships, intimacy issues and much more. For me, this fear manifested itself in my being so afraid that if I did anything wrong then people would leave me. This meant that I walked around on eggshells in most relationships, terrified that I would mess up somehow and that when I did, that person would walk out on me. I will explain to you how this fear was developed soon.

Everyone's experiences are different, and everyone is affected by them differently. Something that might seem minor to one person can cause enormous mental pain to another.

As well as in my own life, I have seen this time and time again with the young people that I have been involved with in my mental-health work. I see the lengths that they go to in order to avoid feeling abandoned. However, unfortunately, the things they do can often heighten their emotions and increase their feelings of being a burden to other people, which feeds into their fear of being abandoned. I often see this when I start talking with a young person (typically a young girl) who is struggling with self-harm and suicidal thoughts. Due to how much I am involved with, I am usually unable to reply quickly to their messages, and that can increase their fear that I am going to abandon them. This then leads to them escalating their actions and either severely self-harming or telling me they are about to take their life, in order to 'draw me back in', getting me to engage with them more closely so they feel safe again.

I want to make this perfectly clear: *this does not make them bad people,* at all. This is just the way that they have learnt to respond to their fear of abandonment. In their minds, people can't love them for who they are, but they have seen that when they are in crisis, people show that they care. However, when this does happen and things escalate and they end up in hospital or a respite house, they then look at the people around them who have come to be with them—the parents or friends who have come to the hospital, who have sat there with them until the early hours of the morning—and they start to feel guilty that they put these people through this, and then the feeling of being a burden starts to heighten and the cycle continues. The reason that I know this so clearly and I don't get angry or upset about it is because I have been in this position myself. It is a learnt 'crisis response', which likely started when they were very young.

There was a part of me who was bubbly, fun and energetic, and a part who was strong and could fight through the hardest circumstances. Then there was also the girl who didn't want to live.

I am not a mental-health professional, but I do know that often these behaviours can be rooted in this intense fear of being abandoned. Like I said earlier, when someone who has this fear starts to feel like you might leave them, or that you don't like them anymore, sometimes they will exaggerate or push themselves to a crisis point in a desperate attempt to get you to stick around a little longer. This fear can keep you stuck in a vicious cycle, because it feeds into your beliefs of being unlovable and being a burden.

While your first thought might be 'Wow, how manipulative', I want you to understand that when people start responding like that, they are not thinking with their logical brain. In fact, they are most likely responding through the lens of a childhood experience that scarred them. It could be anything from having watched their parents divorce, to being a six-year-old whose friends told her that she couldn't sit with them anymore. Everyone's experiences are different, and everyone is affected by them differently. Something that might seem minor to one person can cause enormous mental pain to another.

Looking back onto the crisis times of my life, I realised that for as long as I can remember I had an intense fear of being abandoned. I was too afraid to get close to people or let them in to my life fully, because I believed that they would leave me before long. This manifested in a lot of different ways throughout my life, and it is painful to remember the things that I did and the lengths that I went to so that I could try to avoid feeling abandoned.

This kind of feels like an 'expose all' chapter for me, because it is not something that I have often talked about publicly. It was one of the things that took the longest time for me to start to change, and through my teenage years it got played out in some pretty ugly ways.

As I write this book, I am surrounded by the most incredible friends and loved ones, but that hasn't always been the case. To be honest, I don't think I can look back at my earlier life and see any relationships that I had where I was completely genuine, or that lasted longer than a couple of years at best. This was usually not anything to do with the other person, but everything to do with me. If I felt like someone was getting close to me I would automatically begin to assume that they would leave me soon enough—that they would get to know the 'real me' and walk out.

My fear of abandonment would manifest in one of two ways, the first being isolation. You can read more about the second response—crisis mode—in the next chapter. I mean isolation in both the physical 'hiding away' sense, where I would avoid social situations, not go to church and not go out with my friends, and also in the way that I related to people. I would put on a million different masks to try to ensure people didn't see the real me, so that they didn't find out how broken I really was. I was afraid that if they knew then they would hate me as much as I hated me.

My different masks would come out for different people. With my friends I would be loopy, energetic and fun. I remember going bowling once with a group of people and was really loud the whole night. I was laughing with my friends while we all learnt how terrible I was at bowling, acting extremely happy and fun. The reality, however, was that I had just been released from hospital the day before for self-harming. The friends I was with had no idea and I didn't want to tell them because I didn't want them to think any less of me.

If I felt like someone was getting close to me I would automatically assume that they would leave me soon enough—that they would get to know the 'real me' and walk out.

I made myself become the person I thought they wanted to have around them because in my mind 'no one wants to be around a downer'. I also just didn't want them to know that I had this whole side of me that was broken. I needed them to think I had it all together so that, just for a short moment, I felt like I actually was that person. I could pretend that I wasn't dealing with these major mental-health issues.

However, I used a different mask for those who I looked up to. They saw me as strong, a fighter and a warrior. They also didn't see the current crisis points of my life, they only knew about the past stuff. This helped me feel like I was through it all, that I was on the other side of it.

But then there were those who I trusted, those who I wanted to tell everything to but was too afraid. These are the people who saw a very broken, hurt and suicidal girl. They are the people who would get calls from me, crying and saying I wanted to die. They would have to physically fight me to take away the suicide methods that I had in my possession. These were the people who I was most afraid of losing.

Looking back, while these were all masks, I think they were all a part of me. There *was* a part of me who was bubbly, fun and energetic, and there *was* a part of me who was strong and could fight through the hardest circumstances. Then there was also the girl who was battling her own mind daily, the girl who didn't want to live. For a long time I just assumed that my identity was 'suicidal girl', but that was never the case. There was always this fun-loving warrior girl inside of me.

I think it was easier for me to separate the different masks I presented to different people because it meant that I could always escape my reality and be 'someone else'. But using these masks always made me feel so alone. Everyone I knew only saw one part of me, and I felt like they only liked me or stuck around for the one part they saw. I couldn't let anyone see all of it, because then they would hate me as much as I hated me. I was trapped in my own behaviour, and I had no idea how to get out of it.

CHAPTER TWELVE

Crisis response

People often ask me if I actually wanted to die every time that I was suicidal and the honest answer is no. When I was younger, I was suicidal because of external situations and things that had happened to me, and the suicide attempts were often driven by thoughts like, 'I don't want to die but I can't keep living like this and so this seems like the only option.' However, as I got older and my fear of being abandoned started coming out, my suicidal tendencies switched to *really* wanting to die, because I wholeheartedly believed that everyone would be better off without me. This was because I was living in a constant crisis state, unable to regulate my emotions, meaning that I had more and more hospital visits and crisis-team interventions. The more this happened, the more I felt like I was always on the verge of losing everyone who cared about me and that they really would be better off with me dead.

The isolation response I discussed above is probably a lot more common and better understood than my other response to my fear of abandonment. That response was to always live in this 'crisis mode', because I felt that if I was in crisis, that would make people care about me, even if it was just momentarily. For a long time, I thought I was the only one who felt this way, but as I began to work in the area of mental health I discovered how common it actually is, and how destructive it is.

To explain, the 'crisis response' is basically where a person feels the need to live in a high state of crisis all the time—on the verge of suicide, self-harming, their emotions out of control and in desperate need of help. This means that people around them show them momentary love or care (which is often missing, or has previously been missing, from their lives).

If someone is willing to play with life and death in order to get the

help they are seeking, then we as a society have a real issue.

This may be more common nowadays because we live in a society that teaches people that they are not important or not heard unless they are in crisis. I couldn't tell you the number of times I have seen actively suicidal people turned away from hospital by systems that portray, 'Come back when you have tried to kill yourself.' It's like telling people they should just cheer up when they disclose that they are depressed. Society's current response is basically telling people that unless they have tried to take their lives or they are in a 'bad enough' state then they are not worthy of or eligible for help.

This response from society will hopefully give you an understanding of why I tried (and failed) to take my life 14 times. As I have said, when I was younger I don't think that I actually wanted to die, but I didn't want to keep living with the pain I was carrying. I remember asking for help when I was younger, but being told that I wasn't 'bad enough'. Yet at the same time I would see other people around me crumble and hurting themselves, then see people run to their rescue. I would watch in school as a girl cut herself in the classroom, then all the teachers ran to her and she immediately got seen by the school counsellor.

I couldn't tell you the number of times I have seen actively suicidal people turned away from hospital by professionals who say, 'Come back when you have tried to kill yourself.'

At this time, I was in a lot of mental pain but I didn't know how to ask for help, so I learnt that this was one way to get it. I started self-harming, and while the majority of the time I was hurting myself in places nobody could see and was doing it because I just needed to feel some kind of release, the idea that 'If I need help then I need to escalate my actions' ingrained itself in my brain.

So as I got older, I adopted this mindset of 'Maybe if I hurt myself, then people will know how much I am struggling and will help me.' For those of you who are reading this and thinking 'How could you do that?', I want you to understand that this is way more common than you would think. People who have tried to take their life multiple times often know how far to go to hurt themselves, but not die. Shock statement, I know—I did say this would be a 'tell all'-type chapter. Once again, that doesn't make them bad people—in fact, I think it is really sad that we have taught young people that doing something like this is the only way to get help, that it is the only way to get other people to maybe, just maybe, understand how much pain you are in. Here's the thing: if someone is willing to play with life and death in order to get the help they are seeking, then we as a society have a real issue.

There were quite a few times when I tried to take my life, not knowing if I would die or not. Even if I knew I probably hadn't done enough or done it right, there was always the possibility that I would die. And to be honest, I was OK with that. I was OK with dying. I was OK with living, too, but I knew

I couldn't keep living the way that I was. Death felt like the only option, because it felt like things could never change.

However, this was dangerous, because as I said earlier, this mindset only lasted so long before it turned into really wanting to die. Looking at everyone around me—those who had been dragged to the hospital, who had received goodbye messages or sat with me in crisis—I thought that they wanted me dead. They might not know it at the time, but eventually they would see that their lives were better with me gone.

This led me to waking up every single day thinking about suicide. Walking around and looking at trees and just seeing myself hanging in them. Researching the most painless yet effective ways to die. Wondering how quickly people would move past my death. This became my reality for five years.

*

These thoughts and my fear of being abandoned heightened when I met

Wayne and Libby and became close to them—not because of anything they did, but because they became my family and I was so afraid of losing that.

I was so used to people leaving me when they got to know 'who I really was'. People who I had confided in in my later years of high school began to tell me I was 'too much to handle' and always ended up walking away. This was also evident by the number of people who felt they couldn't have me in their homes any more because of my crisis state. I can understand why, because it is full-on living with someone who is suicidal—you don't know if you are going to wake up to find them dead or missing. But moving around from house to house increased my feelings of being 'too much' for people and increased my fear that everyone would leave me.

As part of my recovery, I had to retrain my brain—to change the way I thought and reacted to things.

As I got closer to Wayne and Libby, and they got to see more and more of my brokenness, I started living permanently on edge, waiting for them to leave me too—waiting for them to realise that I was a mess and too hard to handle. I saw them through the filter of my past, which meant that at times I would act like that scared kid, out of fear that they would abandon me.

I remember one time when I was working at a church conference and Wayne and Libby were both singing. As the stage manager I had to send the band and vocalists onto the stage for the start time, and I accidentally sent them on something like 30 seconds too early. As soon as I realised I started freaking out, feeling like they were going to hate me for it. I had screwed up and they knew it. After the session finished, I avoided them backstage and tried to go to the dressing room to grab my stuff and leave. I felt like such a failure.

As I was walking out of the dressing room I saw Wayne walking towards me, so I put my head down and tried to walk past quickly. He grabbed me and hugged me and said, 'Great job tonight.' *He hadn't even realised what had happened.* Yet my brain had gone from 'I have made a mistake' to 'I *am* a mistake'. Crazy, eh? But this happened a lot—whenever I felt I had done something wrong, whether it be something as little as what I have described above, or trying to kill myself, I always expected them to just get up and leave.

This thinking saw me attempting to hurt or kill myself several times—going in and out of hospital and living in crisis mode, because I believed that if there was something going on with me, then they would still care about me and not walk away. I didn't believe that they could ever love me for who I was, but if something bad or serious was going on then I could still feel loved, even if it was just for a moment.

I remember one night I had spent about four hours crying in my bedroom, writing suicide notes. In all honesty, I can't actually remember what triggered me this day, but I do remember the internal battle. I didn't want to die, but I was in so much pain. Yet I felt I couldn't ask for help. I didn't know how to just pick up the phone and say 'I'm struggling', because when I was younger, saying something like that just got you pushed aside with a 'You will be fine'.

I was so overwhelmed by my emotions that I just got in my car and drove to a cliff near my house. I got out of the car, climbed the barrier and sat on the edge. Half of me wanted to jump, half of me wanted to get help. Now, I know I could have just reached out when these emotions and thoughts first kicked in, but I didn't know how to, so instead I sat on the edge of this cliff for about 20 minutes.

Eventually I decided to pick up the phone and message Wayne and Libby, saying I was on the edge of this cliff and I didn't know what to do anymore. After talking to them on the phone for about half an hour I had calmed down a bit and managed to walk back to my car.

I now know that I could have called them right at the beginning of the day to say I was feeling bad, and they would have been there just as much as they were as I was on the edge of the cliff, but my past hadn't taught me that that would happen.

As part of my recovery, Wayne, Libby and Esther, as the people closest to me, started to help me retrain my brain—to change the way I thought and reacted to things. This was hard, because letting them in to this extent meant I still spent a lot of time being terrified that they would get up and leave. Every time I trusted them a little bit more put me at more risk of being hurt. But let me tell you this before I continue—*they are all still here.*

*

This response and way of acting—going from crisis to crisis—was something I had done all through my teenage years. I had lived literally for years in a state of crisis, believing that at least that way I wouldn't feel alone all the time.

My fear of abandonment and my behaviours around it were a huge contributor to the core beliefs that you read about in the first few chapters. I knew what I was doing was wrong. I thought that I was just wasting people's time and that I really was a burden to them. Fear of abandonment can often help drive these beliefs and for me, that is exactly what it did.

The extent that I would go to in order to avoid being abandoned was huge. And in all honesty, the things I would do and the way I would respond played into my suicidal tendencies a lot. I knew what I was doing to people, and I knew that I was hurting people, and so often when I would be suicidal these stories would run through my mind. It is crazy looking back now to see that my mind would take the smallest things and use them to confirm my beliefs, as a protective mechanism against getting hurt.

However, these beliefs and behaviours were not something that I was born with, or something that just started happening for no reason. Something was driving it, and it was only recently that I discovered what the root cause was.

CHAPTER THIRTEEN

Cast aside

In mid-2017 I had a dream. In it something had happened to me in the middle of the night, and I had run to Wayne and Libby's house for help. I ran down their driveway in the dark and knocked at their door. Wayne answered the door, standing there in his dressing gown. But he didn't look friendly and welcoming like he usually did—he looked angry.

He came out of the house and slammed the door shut behind him. He told me to go away and never come back. I fell to the ground and watched him walk back inside, shut the door behind him and turn off the lights. I sat on the ground, leaning up against the fence, crying, pulling my knees into my chest and rocking back and forth ... Then I woke up.

Let me make this very clear—this was a dream, it didn't actually happen, in fact Wayne is the complete opposite and would never act like that. But when

I woke up I remember thinking 'What the heck was that about?' I tried to shake it off but I couldn't. It was so bizarre—I don't usually remember my dreams, and I had certainly never had one like that before. I felt so uneasy and confused. I hadn't been struggling with suicidal thoughts for the last couple of years and mentally I was in a pretty good place. My relationship with Wayne and Libby was going really well and they had become really loving parents to me. I had no fear of them—they are probably the most loving and gentle people that I know! The dream had been so crazy and so far from the truth that I struggled to understand why my unconscious had created it.

I thought about it all day, and in the afternoon I sent a message to Libby explaining the dream, in the hope that she might be able to help me figure out why this had affected me so much. Libby quickly messaged back, saying, 'Maybe it is your unconscious mind showing your fear that we will abandon you.'

As soon as I read that text I realised that that was exactly what had happened. While I had become really close to Wayne and Libby and considered them family, my subconscious was still putting up a guard, afraid that they would walk away from me. We were closer than we had ever been, and closer than I had probably been to anyone, which to me meant that they could hurt me even more than before. The fear of losing them was still in the back of my mind, especially because at this point of my life I had stopped living in a crisis state. Now that I wasn't in and out of hospital and having drama after drama, it would be a lot easier for them to leave me.

I had been thinking a lot about this for a few months. I hadn't ever really lived a life free of mental illness and crisis before, and because my brain had always told me people could only ever love me when I was in crisis, I was sure that soon they would think I didn't need them any more and would leave.

To be honest, I think that a lot of people who are struggling with mental-health issues fear freedom more than they do living with the illness. I am not speaking for everyone, but I know that for me, I wanted to live without the suicidal thoughts and feelings, but I didn't want to live without the control of knowing that at any point I could take my life if I needed to. I didn't want to live without the relationships that were built upon my being in crisis. So when I finally did fight to be free, the fear of losing people, and especially the relationship I had built with Wayne and Libby, remained for a long time.

A lot of people who are struggling with mental-health issues fear freedom more than they do living with the illness. I wanted to live without the suicidal thoughts and feelings, but I didn't want to live without the control of knowing that at any point I could take my life if I needed to.

As I sat and pondered this on the day after the dream, I also began to think back on *why* I was so afraid. Why *was* I so scared of being abandoned?

I was suddenly brought back to a moment when I was three years old, a moment that in all honesty my mind had totally blocked out for years—maybe because I was only young when it happened, or maybe because I was trying to protect myself. The details around it are hazy, but I remember staying at my biological dad's house that night, and wetting the bed. I remember my dad's response being extreme—he was really angry—but I couldn't remember exactly what his anger looked like, only the feeling of being scared and sensing that I had done something very wrong.

The next day I went to daycare. From what I recall it was a pretty normal day—I played games, jumped on the trampoline and ran around with the other kids. However, my Child, Youth and Family files say that this was also around the time that my behaviour became over-sexualised and fearful.

As the day came to an end, my dad came to pick me up. I'm not sure of the interactions that took place when he got to daycare, but I do remember seeing him walk up to the gate, and then I got taken inside. Then my dad walked away and never came back. And when I say 'never came back', I don't mean he would call every now and then or anything like that—he was just *gone,* never to be seen or heard from again, to the point where I wouldn't have recognised him even if I was walking down the street and he walked past.

I never really knew exactly what happened that day, and to be honest I am not sure if I will ever really know the full truth. I have asked different people who were there that day and others who knew him and have found out that when he arrived, the people at daycare knew he wasn't supposed to be there because there was some kind of custody battle going on. They called the police and then the police took him away, without him being able to see me.

Having my dad leave that day broke me in more ways than I could ever imagine. It made me feel like I had done something wrong—that he had left because of me, because I had screwed up and wet the bed. I thought that if I hadn't messed up then maybe he would still be here. This formed a strong and horrible belief in me that there was something wrong with me, that I was the reason he had left. Even after I found out that he had actually been taken by police that day, I was left with the knowledge that he still chose not to contact me again. He knew I existed but he chose to never once try to reach out, which, in my mind, meant there had to be something wrong with me.

Growing up without my dad seemed somewhat normal for a while. I guess it was all that I knew. My mum and dad had broken up when I was a baby, so when everything happened when I was three years old they were both already in other relationships. I had still been seeing my dad every now and then until I was three, but after that there was absolutely nothing.

Having my dad leave broke me in more ways than I could ever imagine. It made me feel like I had done something wrong—that he had left because of me.

A few years ago I got in touch with one of my half-sisters from my dad's side. I had known her when I was a toddler, but nothing really after that.

We got talking on Facebook and I began to ask her about our dad and if she knew what had happened to him. She is five years older than me so had a better memory of him, and she said that she remembered one day when my dad and my mum were having a huge fight and we had to hide in the closet while it all happened. I don't remember any of this, but she said that it sounded pretty brutal from my dad's side.

She knew a lot more about our dad than any of us, as he had kept in contact with her when she was younger and had been in and out of her life for years. I had never understood why he didn't keep in touch with me. I grew up questioning everything, thinking it was my fault that he was gone.

When I started school, I remember watching lots of kids come in the school gates with their dads, or their dads coming to sports games or activity days that we had. I hated watching them—I felt alienated, like I was the only one without a dad. And my brain told me that it had to be because of me—because I wasn't good enough, or pretty enough, or I wasn't a good daughter. I remember spending days wondering what it would be like to have a dad, but then also wondering what I did to make mine leave.

I don't remember what was going on at home at this point, but I remember feeling really unseen and like I didn't matter. My half-sister had a lot going on, and mental-health services were in and out of the house all the time. It felt like she always needed my mother's attention and that I was kind of swept aside. This may not have been a true reflection of what was going on at home, but it was how I felt.

This half-sister was from my mother's side, and she still had her dad. I remember driving up to the town he lived in so my sister could go and stay with him for weekends, and I would be so jealous—jealous that she had a dad, and jealous that he wanted to see her. It made me feel like I was cast aside. **Now I know a bit more about my dad, I know that I was actually really lucky that he was totally taken from my life when I was three, and that he then chose to stay out of my life as I grew up.**

I always knew that my dad had other kids—I knew a couple of them when I was a younger but then we lost contact. Through the half-sister who I contacted on Facebook I discovered that there are actually around 14 of us. Fourteen kids and yet none of us knew our dad! I still don't know all of them, but we have found a few (or they have found us). One of them is a six-year-old girl—her mother contacted me on Facebook after she saw me on TV, saying that I was her daughter's half-sister. Another person contacted the half-sister who I had been speaking to in 2018, saying that she thought she was our sister, and that she was now in foster care.

It broke my heart to know that there are 14 of us (and probably more, to be honest) who are all feeling the same thing. Fourteen of us who grew up without a father, who have asked why they weren't good enough for him or why he didn't stick around.

Being 24 now and knowing a bit more about my dad, I know that I was actually really lucky that he chose to stay out of my life. However, growing up believing that there was something wrong with me and that he left because of me was one of the hardest things I have ever had to deal with.

CHAPTER FOURTEEN

Developed fear

My dad leaving me at a young age also led to that pattern of 'crisis' behaviour. It is what developed my belief that messing up would make people leave, but also started to teach me that if I lived in 'crisis mode' then people would stay.

One day when I was about six, I was on a school field-trip with my class to a beach. I remember walking beside my teacher and another kid in my class. This kid was talking about how her dad was taking her on a 'daddy-daughter' date after school, and she was really excited about it. She then turned and asked me what my dad's name was and what he did.

At that stage I didn't know the answer to either of those questions, but I flashed back to a joking conversation that my half-sister and I had had a couple of weeks prior. We didn't talk about my dad often—to be honest, the majority of our conversations were just us fighting—but I remembered her saying that my dad had drowned. I don't know if she'd said this to try to protect me from remembering that he left or if she was just trying to make me feel bad, but I'd taken it on board. Without a second thought, I blurted out, 'My dad drowned.'

I remember my teacher looking down at me and grabbing me to hug me. As this little six-year-old kid, in that moment I felt so much love. I felt like I mattered and my little brain went 'Oh, I like it when people care about me like this.'

I started to believe that while people could never love me for who I was, they could show me some kind of love if there was something going wrong.

That one incident, that one moment, started to form a habit that grew to nearly destroy me as a teenager. It implanted a new belief that would work tightly with my fear of abandonment: that if I always had something going on, then people wouldn't leave. I started to believe that while people could never love me for who I was, they could show me some kind of love if there was something going wrong.

I believe this is one of the biggest things that formed many of the patterns in my life, the kind of patterns that would see me hurting those around me and eventually feeling like a horrible person. These actions and feelings created something inside of me that I hated and pushed me to isolate myself, putting up walls and wearing masks. I believed that no one could ever love me for who I was, which affected my friendships, but I could get love and attention if something was going wrong and I seemed like I needed help and support.

Looking back at every friendship that I had had through my childhood and teenage years, it makes a lot of sense now—why I would do anything to try to stop people leaving me, why I felt like I was always the problem and that I wasn't good enough. I was acting like a three-year-old who wet the bed and then watched her dad walk out and never come back.

As a kid I had assumed my mistake of wetting the bed was the reason that my dad chose to leave. It wasn't until years later, when I read my Child, Youth and Family files, that I discovered that there was a whole legal battle going on behind the scenes that I wasn't aware of. My dad didn't leave because I made a mistake, he left for a million other reasons—one being that he wasn't fit to be a parent.

As I began to unravel these feelings that I had held on to my whole life, I discovered that so much pain had been rooted in my dad abandoning me. So, of course, once I had a reliable, positive father figure like Wayne in my life, it would make sense that I would be so afraid of losing him. Like any kid, I would have looked up to my dad. I probably would have adored him. And he left me.

*

When I was in the psych ward in 2015, following my suicide attempt when I had met Constable Campbell, I decided that I wanted to try to get in touch with my father. At this stage I had been in the ward for about a month, and to be honest I think I just wanted answers. I wanted to know what had really happened. Why he didn't want me. I wanted to know where he had been all these years, and why he had never bothered to contact me.

It was all very spontaneous—I didn't talk to anyone about it, I just acted on impulse and started to try and find him as I sat in my room on the ward. I knew a family friend who knew someone else who knew my dad, and eventually I managed to get a cell-phone number for him. (Let me just say, by the way, that while you are in a psych ward is *never* a good time to try to re-establish a relationship or try to get answers about your life and issues—something I learnt after the fact!) Part of me knew it wasn't a good idea, but I went ahead and did it anyway. I was so determined to find answers. I think I wanted to try to find out anything that could help me understand why I was in a psych ward—how my life had gone so horribly wrong. Part of me was hoping that he would give me those answers.

I remember sitting in my room in that ward typing text messages and then deleting them, over and over again. I couldn't tell you how many times that I did this, but eventually I built up the courage to press send. I don't remember exactly what the message said, but it was something along the lines of telling him who I was, asking if he remembered me and saying that I wanted to talk.

Contacting my dad allowed me to close a door—a door I had kept open, hoping maybe one day he would come back and we would have a relationship.

A few hours later, my phone rang. It was my dad. My heart started pounding and I didn't know what to do. I threw my phone on my bed and started crying uncontrollably. I hadn't seen or heard from this man since I was three years old, and now he'd just responded to my message by calling me. I was totally freaked out, but I knew I had an opportunity to find out what the heck had happened in my childhood—why my dad left me, and why he had never tried to get in touch with me. Maybe it would help me find justification for why I acted and felt the way I did—basically, why I was the way that I was.

Eventually I picked up the phone and called him back. When he answered and I heard his voice for the first time, shivers sprinted down my spine. I was suddenly filled with so much anger, so much hurt. I began to spit out words, asking him why he left me.

Eventually he started telling me his version of my childhood. My dad had no idea that I had read my CYFS files and that I already knew about the abuse, and his part in it, but I didn't say anything. I just listened to his side of the story—a side that in all honesty I wish I had never heard. To this day I still don't know the full extent of what happened when I was a three-year-old, but what I do know is that I was abused, I was hurt and I was broken.

I sat on the floor of my room in that ward, tears and snot streaming down my face, listening to my father speak. I couldn't say anything, I felt totally choked up and like everything he was telling me was a lie. Hearing his voice gave me flashbacks to when I was a child and took me right back to feeling like that kid again, like a helpless, scared three-year-old.

We had been on the phone for about 15 minutes when Eve, my nurse, walked in and saw me. In my hospital notes it says, 'I found Jazz on the floor crying with her phone on speaker. She looked up and mouthed "help me" and I told her to hang up.'

I was completely traumatised by having spoken to him.

I never heard from him again. I remember talking to Esther after this initial contact and she said, 'Jazz, you are expecting him to do something that he is literally not capable of'—and she was right. I was asking a very broken man who had a pattern of lying to tell me the truth, something that he actually wasn't capable of doing.

However, in saying all of that, I am thankful that I chose to make that call, because while it ended in hurt, it also, in a way, allowed me to close a door—a door I had kept open, hoping maybe one day he would come back and we would have a relationship. It also enabled me to understand that I was actually so much better off without him in my life and I was lucky to have grown up without him. I could stop asking the question 'why', because I finally understood that he was incapable of being a father. That it wasn't me, it wasn't my fault, but he just wasn't cut out for it.

*

I never really understood the effects of my dad leaving me until I met Wayne and became close to him and Libby. He was the first father figure I had known who did not hurt me, the first one that I didn't feel afraid of, and the first who didn't make me feel worthless.

Meeting Wayne enabled me to start to heal from this trauma. I truly believe that it took another father to help fix the damage my own father had done.

I hadn't trusted many men in my life at all. The three men I had in my life who were father-type figures had all sexually abused me and then left. After that, I never really had a father figure in my life. I think I was always subconsciously looking for one, though; I always wanted to have a father and to know what it was like to be loved by a dad.

For me, meeting Wayne enabled me to start to heal from this trauma—from the abuse, from being left and from feeling like I wasn't enough.

Wayne has taught me what it is to be unconditionally loved by a dad. He taught me that I was enough, that I didn't have to earn love or approval. He taught me that I didn't deserve to be abused, and that it was possible for me to be safe. In all honesty, he restored my faith in men. Both he and Libby were key parts of my healing and ensuring that I knew that no matter what was going on, or what I was doing or had done, I was loved—no strings attached.

For other people, this may be a friend, a counsellor or another family member. It may even be a pet, or faith. Healing can come from all angles.

CHAPTER FIFTEEN

Fear of three

Because of the things that happened to me when I was a young child, and my reactions to them, as I grew up I was never able to maintain strong friendships. I guess it was because I would never let anyone past surface level. I would put guards up and I never trusted people, because I feared that they would either hurt me or leave me. I lived feeling like I wasn't good enough, fearful that soon they would figure that out and then walk away.

Another fear which grew out of my core beliefs and caused me to act in negative ways was the fear of being in a group of three people. I have always hated being in a group of three friends or any group of three people. I would always believe the other two people secretly hated me and were talking about me behind my back.

It was tied in with the belief that I was a burden and I was unlovable, but I knew there was more to it than that.

I always felt the need to confirm that people still liked me. This wasn't a huge thing of literally asking 'So, do you still like me or...?'—I just wanted confirmation through the fact they still wanted to hang out with me. If they would invite me places, message me or just want to hang out then I would be assured that in that moment, we were still friends.

I think part of this came from school, where the girls would be friends with you one day and then talking behind your back the next. I never knew where I stood with them, what I would walk into or who my true friends were (in hindsight, there weren't many ... high school can be pretty rough and catty!). Every time I walked into a room I would assume that the people in it had been talking about me.

There are many things wrong with that kind of thinking and with those kinds of assumptions. By making these assumptions and placing them on my friends, I was filtering them through my own experiences, which wasn't fair on them. It also meant I went into every relationship expecting it to end. I entered every friendship assuming that people didn't actually like me, living on edge and preparing for the day they would hurt me.

*

This fear has taken a long time to shake, and recently I had the opportunity to really think about where it came from. In early 2019 I was walking around Cornwall Park in Auckland with two of my closest friends—something that we try to do every week. We all meet at the entrance of the park, walk down to the café and get some coffee then begin walking the big loop through the park.

This particular day was no different—we met at the entrance, strolled down to get coffee and then began our walk. But while we were walking, something happened that triggered a wave of memories.

One of my friends said something about me—nothing bad, but the tone in which she said it, alongside my other friend laughing with her when she said it, suddenly brought up all of these feelings. In my head I automatically jumped to 'They don't even want me here. I have invaded their walk and they would prefer it if I would just leave.' As these thoughts entered my head I countered them, thinking 'Where on earth did that come from? These are two of my best friends, who have never given me reason to think that they don't like me. Why have I assumed this?'

Then I remembered a chapter I had read in a book that Libby wrote called *Journey,* telling the story of her own life and the battles she overcame. I had read it about a year beforehand. It was a chapter about barricading your thoughts and then trying to find the root cause of them. Basically, the idea of it is trying to capture a negative thought the second that it enters your brain, then trying to figure out where it has actually come from.

I entered every friendship assuming that people didn't actually like me, living on edge and preparing for the day they would hurt me.

Libby gives the example of having these intense thoughts of not being good enough, but never actually knowing why she felt that way. Then one day when this thought came into her mind, she stopped and started to think back to where this belief came from. She went back to being seven years old and having a friend coming over to her house. She was super excited and spent the entire afternoon making a little origami love heart to give to her friend. When her friend arrived, Libby was so excited to give it to her.

After they had played and the girl went home, Libby walked into the kitchen and saw the heart sitting in the rubbish bin. She automatically thought that because her friend had put it in the bin, that meant she was not good enough. So as she got older, she was always second-guessing her worth, until she thought back to that childhood event and worked out where that belief had come from.

Remembering this chapter, I managed to stop myself in that moment and say to myself, 'Push that aside, Jazz, and carry on walking. This is not the reality, and you can figure out why you reacted this way later.'

Once we finished the walk and I got into my car, I started to think about it again, trying to figure out why on earth I had had such a dramatic response to such a small and irrelevant comment. As I did, I had a flashback to a moment when I was seven years old.

I was living on a suburban street in my hometown, Timaru. It was a quiet neighbourhood from what I can remember, with a lot of old people and also a lot of kids my own age. I lived about eight houses down from a park, and I would often go down there and play, as would a lot of the other kids in the neighbourhood.

There were two girls in particular who I became friends with—let's call them Alice and Kelly. Kelly lived in the house behind me, and there was a fence that separated our two back yards. Alice lived two houses down from me, and her back yard also backed onto Kelly's yard.

One day Alice came knocking at my door, asking if I wanted to go down to the park and play with her. I was so excited! I remember asking my mum and then throwing on my shoes and running out the door and joining Alice to walk down to the park.

As we began to walk down the alleyway that ran from our street to the park, I noticed Alice starting to act weird, and as we turned the corner onto the park I saw Kelly standing there. Alice looked over at Kelly and said, 'Oh my gosh, I didn't know you were going to be down here. Jasmine, I don't want to play with you anymore, I want to play with Kelly. You can go home.' Both girls then burst out laughing.

I turned around and bolted back to my house, crying the whole way home. Kelly and Alice had planned that moment. They had planned that Alice would come to my house and pretend that she wanted to play with me. They had planned that Kelly would wait at the park, and that when we arrived they would turn around and tell me that I wasn't wanted.

*

I never understood the effect that moment had on me, or the thought patterns that it created. I didn't even really remember the incident until this conversation with my friends in the park had occurred. No wonder I had so much trouble trusting groups of people, why I always assumed that they didn't actually want me around or that they would hurt me soon enough! As a seven-year-old I couldn't comprehend what was going on. I never told anyone what had happened—I just bottled it up and carried it with me through the rest of my childhood and teenage years.

I had so much trouble maintaining friendships in primary school, mainly because I never trusted anyone. I always assumed that friends were talking about me behind my back, or that they didn't actually care about me. I was always waiting for them to turn around and hurt me.

This, at times, turned me into the bully. I started talking about other kids behind their backs, with the mindset 'If they are talking about this other person with me, then they are not talking about me with them.' This thinking was faulty and destructive and ensured that

I didn't keep any friends at all from school.

When I got to high school I would hop around groups because girls were constantly turning on me—asking me one day to come and sit with them and then the next day telling me to go away. There was a popular group of girls at school (like every high school on the planet) that I was friends with in the first few weeks of school, then they kicked me to the kerb pretty quickly. Then there was another group of girls that I became friends with, about seven of us, but the drama in that group was worse than a teenage TV show! Every day the situation was different—people who I had thought were my friends would suddenly not talk to me, and then a week later would act like my best friends again. To say it was confusing would be an understatement.

I was so determined to pretend to be someone different than who I was because I thought maybe then people would accept me and be friends with me.

It also meant I was trying so hard to fit in and to not be hurt that I lost who I was in the process. It was a very subtle thing, but something that, looking back, also destroyed many of my earlier friendships. I was so determined to pretend to be someone different than who I was because I thought maybe then people would accept me and be friends with me. My friends would never know that I was struggling and I would never let them see anything except a bubbly, fun girl who didn't seem to have a care in the world.

I was so afraid of being judged, but I also wanted to try to fake some kind of normality. Don't get me wrong—there were definitely times when I was genuinely happy, bubbly and outgoing. There were times when I would have a great day, when I would excel in school and behave like a normal kid. But there were also days when I felt so alone, so unwanted and so broken. A lot of the time I felt like I was the only person going through this.

I didn't really talk to anyone about what was going on. However, when I was in year 10, I had a drama teacher named Miss Bennett. I really loved drama class and I was really good at it. Miss Bennett became a bit of a safety net for me. I would often stay after class and talk to her about what was going on at school, and if girls were bullying me and harassing me then I would go and sit in the drama room at lunchtime. She was really supportive and helped me a lot when it came to conflict management and ensuring that I felt like I could come back to school the next day. If I had had people like Miss Bennett in my life through my entire school years I think that life could have been a little bit different and a little less lonely. Most teachers did care, but a lot of them just didn't have time for me.

The good news is, once I had identified this thought pattern and the assumptions I had, I knew I needed to address them right away. I was working with a counsellor at this stage, which helped a lot, and I had also learnt tools myself through my own experiences so I knew I needed to not dwell on this and address it immediately.

It wasn't something I could just 'switch off', but every time my mind would say 'maybe they don't want me here', I would stop it right away and remind myself that I am not seven anymore. My friends today are not those two girls, Kelly and Alice, and they are not going to reject me.

It's important to remember that healing and retraining your brain doesn't happen overnight and we are always learning. For me, identifying the underlying experiences and issues was key in allowing me to move forward and experience lasting change.

CHAPTER SIXTEEN

Fight the fears

I was very intentional in including these chapters within this book. I remember fighting my fears for so long, thinking that I was the only one who struggled with them, and that I was the only person who felt like I had to have drama going on for people to not abandon me. However, as I mentioned earlier, since I have become an advocate for mental health I can't tell you how many young girls I have come across who have responded this exact way. These girls are living in crisis mode, believing that the only way to feel loved is to be on the edge all the time. (Interestingly, so far, it has only been girls who I have seen doing this, maybe because girls are more likely to try to talk about things compared to guys, but also I don't get a lot of young guys contacting me for help.)

I see them creating Instagram accounts to share photos of themselves in hospital, and pretending to have stitches for cuts that didn't exist. I see them feeling the need to send goodbye messages in order to draw closer people that they feared they were going to lose. I see such self-hatred and fear of people leaving in all of these girls—the kind of self-hatred and fear that I once had. They know that at times they are lying to me, or probably feel that they are wasting my time, but now, being on the other side of it, I realise that I have never once felt like I wanted to leave them. I know they are hurting and I can see past their behaviours to understand that there is actually just a very broken and scared person behind them—someone who needs to know that they are loved no matter what is going on in their life and that people won't leave them.

You are not a burden, and you are not alone. Responding in this way is not helpful, but it doesn't make you crazy. You don't have to keep living like that, and it is possible to live without the constant fear of being abandoned.

Watching and talking with these young girls makes me think a lot about my history and experiences. I remember at the time I was going through this thinking how much those around me hated me for acting like this. Now I understand that people really did care, they wanted to help me and they loved me no matter what was going on. I also see now that at times they may not have known what to do or how best to respond, that they may have felt overwhelmed themselves and so pulled away, but that definitely did not mean that they didn't care or that they hated me.

If you see yourself in the behaviour I've been describing, I want you to know that you are not a burden, and that you are not alone. You probably already know that responding in this way is not helpful, but it doesn't make you crazy. You don't have to keep living like that, and it is possible to live without the constant fear of being abandoned.

*

There were many practical things that I did to begin working through the process of fighting my fears and start healing. A lot of it was interlinked with the practical things I did to fight my core beliefs that we talked about at the start of the book, because this fear of abandonment and those beliefs often stood side by side.

The first thing I did to start overcoming my fear of being abandoned was to identify the people who I worried about leaving me the most. These people were my closest friends and those who had been journeying with me for years. There were two groups of people that fell into this:

- my family figures, who I filtered through my experiences of my father and my other close family, and
- my close friends, who I filtered through the experience of being bullied by Kelly and Alice and my high school peers.

For these two groups of people, the practical things that I did varied, because although being afraid of losing family and losing friends were two different fears that had kind of spiralled into one, I felt I needed to approach challenging them in a slightly different way.

When it came to the family figures of Wayne, Libby and Esther, I had to become so intentional about barricading my thoughts. The core-beliefs list that I talked about in chapter 9 was one of the ways that I did that, because not only did it help break those beliefs, it also helped reinforce the fact that these people were still there in my life, staying alongside me. Although my mind would constantly tell me they would leave, and I spent so long preparing for that, they never did.

On that core-beliefs list I would write not only the things they said, but also the things they did that showed the truth about our relationship and the fact that they were not going to leave me. Things like them still being in my life years after I first thought they would leave; like the fact that they really had seen me at my worst and they still chose to be there and to fight for me. Alongside the list, I also fought through my fears with my decisions, choosing to barricade my thoughts when they would run to 'they will leave me'.

I was choosing to trust them over what my mind was telling me. I was making the decision to reach out to them despite my mind freaking out; deciding to not act in extreme ways to try to get them to stay but to simply trust that they were not going anywhere. A lot of my freedom in this area lay within my decisions, something that I will go into detail on a little later. **One day you will be able to make it through every day without second-guessing everybody's motives, and live a life free of fear.**

So much of my pain, insecurity and fear were instilled into me by 'father figures' who left me and abused me. Wayne chose to step into the gap for me. He began to show me what it was to have a father, and slowly but surely the pain started to disintegrate. It was a long and hard process, and both he and Libby walked with me through it every single step of the way.

I remember being so confused about why they were still here—why did they care? These two had seen me at my worst in the psych ward, drugged up and without hope. They saw me running away, breaking down, ending up in hospital and then pushing them away. Every time my mind would run to 'they don't want you around', I would have to barricade my thinking and come back to reality, saying to myself, 'Jazz, have they left you yet? No. Have they ever indicated that they would leave you? No. Is it fair of you to be filtering them through your past experiences? No. They are not the same people who abandoned you as a toddler like your dad did. They love you.'

This fear isn't something that just magically goes away one day—it takes hard work, consistency and truth to challenge and change it.

This was something I had to do and remind myself of frequently over several years. This fear isn't something that just magically goes away one day—it takes hard work, consistency and truth to challenge and change it. I lived on edge for so long, waiting for them to one day turn around and say, 'We can't handle you, Jazz', but that day never came. Instead, they consistently showed me love in the kind of way that challenged every belief that I had built up over many years.

*

I also had to carry these positive beliefs over into my friendships. I used the same technique of being intentional with my thoughts, reminding myself that my friends now are not Kelly and Alice—they are people who love me, care about me and won't leave me stranded in a park. This meant learning to barricade my thoughts every time I was with them and my mind would say 'they don't want me here' or 'they are just here because they feel they have to be'. It meant being the one to reach out to them and asking if they wanted to hang out. It meant understanding that their responses might not always be what I wanted or needed, and not to take that personally.

I fought through my fears with my decisions, choosing to barricade my thoughts when they would run to 'they will leave me'.

I also learnt how to find good-quality friends, the kind who are genuine, trustworthy and don't care about your status, how much money you have or if you have the latest things. For me, these were the people I found by choosing to let my guard down little by little. It didn't take long to see the ones who wouldn't stick around and find the ones who I could trust.

Living your life believing that everyone has negative intentions or thoughts about you is exhausting. It takes work and consistency to begin to retrain your brain, but believe me, one day you will be able to make it through every day without second-guessing everybody's motives, and live a life free of fear.

CHAPTER SEVENTEEN

Straight talking

When I look back, there is one incident that I think really helped to get me past the belief that I had to have something going on to be momentarily loved and to avoid people leaving me, once and for all. It was a conversation I had with Esther in 2015—she's good at these life-changing conversations, I tell you!—and it is one that I remember every single detail of. At the time I was still really struggling with suicidal tendencies, but after this conversation I found the strength to really battle my way out of the unnecessary drama and stop living in crisis mode.

She had texted me a couple of days earlier, asking to catch up. Remember in high school when a teacher would ask to see you after class and your mind would immediately think of every single thing you had ever done wrong? Well, that is what it was like for me every time someone asked me to catch up, even if it was just wanting to hang out as friends! I would always jump to the worst conclusion. When I got this message I assumed that she was angry with me about something, or had found out that I had screwed up in some way.

Anyway, Esther and I organised to meet up at a coffee shop in a mall down the road from my house. We arrived and bantered for a while, and then she began to sway the conversation to the real reason she wanted to catch up. She was about to untangle all of the lies I had told as a result of my fear of abandonment—the lies I told because I believed that it was the only way that people would momentarily love me, the only way to try to keep people from leaving me. Lies like telling people I had been hospitalised for a medical issue, when in fact it was because I had hurt myself. I was sure I was the only one telling these sorts of lies, but now I see that this behaviour is unfortunately so common among young people.

Esther sat there asking me questions—that she really already knew the answers to—and began to untangle the entire web I had spun. I remember sitting in my chair bawling my eyes out, right in the middle of the mall—I didn't care who was around. I felt so exposed and worthless, convinced that now Esther would leave me for sure.

However, as we got to the end of what felt like an extremely long and painful conversation, Esther did something that I did not expect. She stood up and said, 'Oh, I need to go shopping! Wanna come with me to Kmart?'

I was so sure that Esther would want to run from me right away and never speak to me again—so why was she now inviting me to go shopping with her? How did she not hate me? Why was she not leaving me? I cautiously went with her and did some shopping, and then when it eventually came time to go home she hugged me and said 'Love you!' before she left.

I remember going home and crying my heart out all night, believing that one of the only people at that stage in my life who I respected and trusted would never want anything to do with me again. I was still so sure that Esther wouldn't talk to me again—I mean, she probably just asked me to go shopping because she wanted to make sure I wasn't going to run off and do something stupid, right? Now she was free to just leave me and had every reason to do so.

But she didn't. The next day, she was still there. The next week, the next year, she was still there.

It wasn't an overnight fix of 'now I don't need to create drama to be loved', but it did help change my response pretty quickly. For the next year I still struggled with suicidal tendencies and was in and out of the psych ward, but by this stage it wasn't a ploy for drama. That conversation with Esther helped me understand that people loved me for who I was, not for what was going on.

Don't let your fear of abandonment steal your ability to fight for freedom.

What I want you to understand about this conversation is that Esther managed to do it in a way that started the destruction of my belief that I had to have all of this drama going on for people to care. It was the beginning of shaking off my fear of being abandoned, because I could see that now Esther knew the darkest parts of me and she still hadn't gone anywhere.

*

This kind of conversation is something that I encourage people to have with their loved ones if they know that they are responding in the same way that I once was. Ensure you do it in the way that Esther did for me—in a loving, non-judgemental way—and then try to do something afterwards with that person that is not related to the conversation, so that they can understand that you still care. Show them that these actions do not define them as a person, but are simply a result of childhood brokenness and fears that can be overcome. **It wasn't an overnight fix of 'now I don't need to create drama to be loved', but this conversation did help change my response pretty quickly.**

In order for a conversation like this to be beneficial there are a few things you need to do to ensure that it doesn't escalate the situation. First of all, have it in a neutral environment, whether it be your house, their house or the hospital (a few of the conversations like this that I have had have taken place in the psych ward, because I know the person will be safe there). Don't go in full blast asking them questions—keep it casual, asking them about their day and anything else you know they like talking about. This will help them to bring their walls down a little bit and remind them that you love them.

The last time I had a conversation like this, I brought up the subject about 15 minutes into our get-together by asking how the girl's stitches were. I already knew that she hadn't needed stitches, but she had texted me saying she needed them after self-harming. She told me they were getting better, and then I looked at her and said, 'I'm going to be honest—I know that you didn't actually have stitches and you didn't need to be moved to hospital like you said. Let me first say that this doesn't mean I don't love you, or I think any less of you at all. I know that this is just a response to something, and I just want to find out what is really going on.'

This girl burst into tears and looked away. She had been faking injuries for a while, texting me saying she was at the hospital when she was really at school, and so on. I had noticed a pattern over a few months and I knew for a fact that she hadn't been telling the truth.

I told her that it made total sense to me that she felt like she needed to say these things to get me to respond or message her. She had needs that she wanted filled and she didn't know how to just message saying she was having a hard day. She believed that the only way I would care was if she had actually hurt herself and was in crisis. (Sound familiar? Exactly what I used to do!)

We sat together and I kept reassuring her, telling her that she didn't need to do these things or lie about anything. I told her that I wouldn't be mad at her for telling me things that were not true, but that I was concerned and wanted her to get the help she really needed.

The conversation went on for about an hour, and when I realised I needed to go, I lightened up our chat by asking her some totally irrelevant questions about movies and TV shows she had seen, and then suggested we go watch a movie together the following week. By the time I left, she seemed a lot calmer.

Reassuring people that you don't hate them and will not leave them is vital, and being able to talk about a future event you could do together will help the person feel like you are not about to walk out of their life for good. This girl and I came up with a code word that she would message me if she was really struggling but didn't know how to say it. The code word was simply 'rock', and she would text it to me instead of saying she was in hospital or coming up with another lie.

This really worked! These conversations are hard, but they can be so worth it if they are done with love.

*

To be completely honest, I think that my fear of abandonment was one of the things that kept me bound to my mental illness more than anything else. Believing that people would only love me or care about me when something was going on or when I was struggling meant that the freedom of living without these fears and behaviours was a terrifying concept. I so badly wanted to live without the suicidal thoughts and crisis behaviour, but I was afraid of living without the momentary sense of being loved that these things brought me. A lot of my close relationships had been built while I was struggling, so I was scared that these people would walk away if I became free of this. I still filtered them through this lens of giving me momentary love and care, despite the fact that they had been there for me for years.

Believing that people would only love me or care about me when something was going on meant that the freedom of living without these

fears and behaviours was a terrifying concept.

Now, I am so thankful that I did continue to fight for freedom, because in doing so I have discovered a new kind of relationship with these people—the kind of relationship where we are simply 'doing life' together, where we can sit and laugh, dream about the future and talk about the adventures of life.

For anyone who is struggling with these same beliefs or fears, remember that you are not your behaviour. You do not have to say or do these things in order for people to love you or care about you. You are worthy of love, and it is time to stop viewing the people who care about you through the filter of your past experiences.

Don't let your fear of abandonment steal your ability to fight for freedom.

HAVING TOUGH CONVERSATIONS

- Ensure you do it in a loving, non-judgemental way—then try to do something afterwards that is not related to the conversation, so that they can understand that you still care.

- Show them that these actions do not define them as a person, but are simply a result of childhood brokenness and fears that can be overcome.
- Talk in a safe environment, whether it be your house, their house or the hospital.
- Don't go in full blast asking them questions—keep it casual at first to help them bring their walls down and remind them that you love them.
- Reassuring people that you don't hate them and will not leave them is vital.
- Being able to talk about a future event you could do together will help the person feel like you are not about to walk out of their life for good.
- These conversations are hard, but can be so worth it if they are done with love.

CHAPTER EIGHTEEN

'Attention-seeker'

'She's just an attention seeker.' If I had a dollar for every time I heard those words, I would be rich.

The idea that people are trying to take their own lives just because they want to get attention is probably one of the biggest misconceptions and most harmful beliefs about poor mental health. It is one phrase that absolutely grinds my gears because of the stigma that society has now attached to it.

From the moment we are born and start developing we need attention. As babies, when we don't get what we need (note I didn't say what we *want*, but what we *need*), we cry until someone picks us up or gives us their attention. Babies cannot thrive without it, and yet we expect teenagers and adults to.

When I was in the depths of my struggle, being told that I was just attention-seeking completely shut me up. It made me not want to ask for help. I would rather sit in my room for hours on end crying and hurting myself than reach out. I was so afraid that people would think that I was just 'attention-seeking'. This belief, forced on me by other people, completely undermined my experiences and the validity of what I was feeling.

People don't just suddenly start attention-seeking—something has happened to them, and they begin reaching out for help and support *because they need it.*

In my mind, if someone said this to me then it meant they didn't think I was really struggling. It threw my guard up and made me feel so belittled.

If we want to get to a place in our society where people are willing to ask for help before a crisis point, then we need to completely reframe the way that we use these two words. People don't just suddenly start attention-seeking—something has happened to them, and because there has been a lack of attention or help somewhere in their life, they begin reaching out for help and support *because they need it.*

When I first started having dark thoughts and uncontrollable emotions I asked for help in the only way I knew how to at that stage. When I was 11, I went to my school teacher after a bullying incident that left me feeling like I wanted to hurt myself, and told her that I was feeling really sad. She turned to me and said, 'Sticks and stones may break my bones but words will never hurt me.'

Oh, how wrong she was. The words others had spoken to me *did* hurt me—in fact, they went on to build the very beliefs that slowly destroyed my life. In that moment with my teacher I was trying to tell her that I was not OK, but I was just pushed aside. She thought that I was exaggerating, and the way that she spoke to me made me feel like I had no right or grounds to feel the way that I did.

This situation taught me that if I was affected by people's words, then *I* was the one who was weak. Being pushed aside and told to essentially 'get over it' made me feel like she thought I was just going to her for attention, when in reality she had no idea how much the behaviour of these girls had affected me.

Eventually, I began to escalate my actions, because it was the only way I knew how to get the help I knew I needed. This escalation involved self-harming, lying and beginning to overwork in school to compensate for what I was feeling.

I was badly bullied in middle school. There was a huge group of kids who hated me and ensured that every single day I knew that was the case. I had tried to tell a teacher what was going on but it was just pushed aside, with them saying 'You just have to ignore it.'

If we want to get to a place in our society where people are willing to ask for help before a crisis point, then we need to completely reframe the way that we use the words 'attention-seeker'.

I remember one day when I was sitting in class and a group of girls were being really horrible to me. They were all sitting behind me on the floor and started throwing scrunched-up paper at me with words like 'ugly' and 'go die' written on them. It felt like these girls' one purpose was to make me miserable, and so as my emotions built I grabbed my bag and ran out of the classroom and down the hall to the bathroom. I locked the door behind me, and as the tears flowed down my cheeks I grabbed a sharp object I had in my bag and I started to hurt myself.

I sat in that bathroom for about half an hour before a teacher walked in and knocked on the door of the stall I was in. I told her to go away but she kept persisting. I eventually covered the places I had hurt myself and opened the door.

I remember the look of concern on her face. She took me up to the office, where I sat and cried, and she saw one of the places I had hurt myself. This teacher then sat with me for the rest of the afternoon. I remember thinking 'Why does she only care now that I have hurt myself? She didn't care when I was being bullied.'

*

Feeling that my cries for help were being continuously ignored by the people at school, I eventually made a decision that no 12-year-old should ever make: the decision to try to end my own life. I remember everything about that night as if it were yesterday, but before I tell you what happened, let me explain the lead-up.

School had been really tough for me. The other girls were in full-force bully mode. People were making statements about me, or whispering in class and then looking back and laughing at me.

One of the girls in my home room had celebrated her dad's birthday the night before and everyone started talking about their dads and the things they did. I started to feel overwhelmed and ran out of the room. We had a few of the senior students in our class for peer support, and one of these students followed me out and started to ask me what was wrong. I wanted to tell her, but I couldn't bring myself to tell her that a) I had been really struggling recently, and b) that my dad had just left one day and I didn't even know who he was. In the moment my brain scattered and I ended up just blurting out that my dad had died when I was younger. I thought that this was easier than trying to explain that he never wanted anything to do with me.

However, being only 12 and not really thinking this through, I got caught in a trap with this lie. I knew that this senior student cared and I wanted to tell her the truth but I didn't know how to.

The guilt of it was eating me up. After about a month she figured it out, and my mum was called into the school office. My mum told them the truth, that my dad was not dead and that I just didn't know him. The school then knew that I had lied, but nobody ever asked why I had done it.

As babies, when we don't get what we need, we cry until someone picks us up or gives us their attention. Babies cannot thrive without it, and yet we expect teenagers and adults to.

Then the staff member Mum spoke to said that I was just an

attention-seeker, and told the students who had tried to help me to not give me the time of day. Her words hit me like a ton of bricks—yes, I had screwed up, but I had done so because my previous plea for help had basically been ignored. I didn't feel like I could even try to defend myself and tell them why I had lied, because I was made to feel like a villain who was just saying these things for attention. The school knew about the bullying, but in their minds they couldn't see how the two could be linked, so I was labelled as the 'troubled kid'.

I was overcome with self-hatred and other strong emotions. This incident, alongside the extreme bullying, made me feel so worthless and like a burden. I felt the world would be better with me gone.

So, a few weeks after that incident I decided to try to end it all. Even though I was young, I knew what suicide was because there had been a few family friends and friends of my older sister who had taken their own lives, and I also had an aunty take her life too. I don't know too much about what actually happened, or why, as it happened before I was born and it wasn't something that my family ever really talked about.

It was around 8.30p.m. and I was sitting in my light-purple-walled bedroom. I had a giant Easter bunny cut-out on my wall and a bright-pink net covering the head of my bed—a classic 12-year-old girl's room back then. I had a small old TV in my room and I sat there watching the *Bones* finale, thinking over the day I had just had. The bullying was continuing and word had spread around the school that I had lied about my dad being dead. Girls were saying things like 'no wonder he wanted nothing to do with you' and 'your parents should have aborted you'. I felt so broken and so alone.

I had access to a suicide method I decided to try using. I don't even know if I wanted to die, I just didn't want to keep living like I was.

I began to feel really unwell. Suddenly I freaked out at the reality of what I had done. I didn't want it to hurt. I ran into my mum's room crying and she asked what had happened. It took me a while—I just stood in the doorway of her room crying, and then I told her that I had taken all of my medication. She replied, 'Why the heck would you do that?'

She got out of bed and we went to the hospital. I didn't ever tell her why I had chosen to try to take my life, we just sat in silence for most of the ride down to the hospital. I remember the look on her face, like she was so angry and could not understand why I would do that. I felt so physically sick, but I also had a huge sinking feeling, looking at my mother's face and realising that she had to drive her daughter who had just tried to kill herself to hospital.

We arrived at the Emergency Department and they made me drink this black tar-like stuff (I now know this is activated charcoal), to line my stomach and stop my body absorbing the poison. As I sat in that hospital room waiting for it to work, I felt like a complete burden. Watching everyone else come in and out of the Emergency Department for serious medical issues and realising that the doctors and nurses had to waste their time on me felt horrible.

The concept of just being an 'attention-seeker' fogged my lens, and I felt like every conversation that I had that night was around people thinking I had just done this for attention. I refused to tell anyone why I had taken the pills, just saying 'I don't know', and after a few hours, when I was medically cleared, they let me go.

To be honest, the outcome of that night does suggest that the professionals really did think I was just attention-seeking. I got referred to a child psychologist for a little bit, and then a few weeks later I was out of the system completely. Isn't it crazy that back then people could believe that you could go from wanting to die one week to being OK just a few weeks later? After those few weeks, the incident was never spoken about again. It wasn't something that was taken seriously, nor was it something health professionals felt should be followed up after I was discharged from their services.

You would think that a 12-year-old trying to commit suicide would raise huge red flags for professionals, but back in 2009, it was merely a case of 'other kids have it worse so she will be fine'. They needed their resources to go to the kids who were trying to take their life *every week,* so I was simply pushed to the side. At that stage they had limited frontline services.

CHAPTER NINETEEN

Changing the script

I often wonder if I had been offered proper help when I first tried to reach out, could I have been saved from falling into my suicidal pattern later on? If I had been told that I mattered, that I was worth helping, would I not have felt the need to escalate my behaviour? I was a young girl who fell through the cracks of our extremely broken system. I wasn't deemed 'bad enough' to get the help I really needed, and instead was pretty much left to try to deal with it by myself. Looking back, I genuinely believe that if I had received proper early intervention, I could have been saved from years of struggling with these thoughts, patterns and behaviours.

Over time my escalation became my identity, and eventually I couldn't escape it. I didn't want to live. I felt I needed to be punished and I battled often with suicidal thoughts. Most people from my early teenage years would tell you that I was this outgoing, bubbly girl, which to a degree I was—but that was because I got really good at hiding what was really going on out of fear of being seen as just an attention-seeker.

As I got further into my teenage years, I heard this expression used about me countless times. The behaviour I've told you about in the previous chapters was all seen as attention-seeking by different people in my life, everyone from professionals to teachers and friends. But when you look past behaviour and look at the 'why', you can begin to understand that there is always a reason behind people's actions.

I responded so extremely to situations out of my fear of being abandoned and out of my beliefs that I was unlovable and a burden. I responded like the three-year-old girl who watched her dad leave and never come back. I responded like the three-year-old girl who was being sexually abused but sworn to secrecy. I responded like the seven-year-old who had been rejected by her friends, and like the 11-year-old who yearned to be accepted by her peers.

People acting like this are not attention-seeking, but help-seeking. That is what people who are struggling with mental-health issues and suicidal tendencies need: help.

I could not tell you how many times in the last couple of years I have seen this behaviour in other young people with mental-health issues, especially young girls. Obviously this is something that boys do struggle with as well, but what I have personally found is that boys are less likely to talk about their emotions. They tend to bottle everything up and then eventually respond with action (which is one of the reasons why males' suicide rates are so high). These are girls who have either tried to ask for help but were ignored and so escalated, or girls who were too afraid to even ask for help because of the known stigma attached to 'attention-seeking'.

If you are thinking 'People would never think that', just read these comments from a news article about a young girl who was found standing on the edge of a bridge, stopping traffic:

Someone go drag that mole back from the edge so traffic can get going. If she was serious she would have done it by now. She just wants attention. Hopefully 50,000 volts worth is being arranged.

If that was my daughter I would have shot her down. How embarrassing.

Just jump, get it over with so that we can get on with our lives.

Getting the point yet? How do you ever expect people, who are struggling, to reach out when these are the kinds of attitudes our society holds about people who are suicidal? I have been that girl on the bridge; I know that if I had read those comments I would never again ask for help when I was in crisis because I would be so afraid that this would be the response I was going to get.

There is such a huge lack of understanding when it comes to mental health and suicidal ideation. Most of the comments on this article actually came from middle-aged people. The people that teenagers are watching and learning off are the ones saying that speaking about mental health is weak, or that people with these problems are just attention-seeking.

These kinds of comments are scrawled all over social media, but they are also made in everyday conversations in our society. We have grown up with the mindset that struggling with mental health makes you a crazy nutter and that talking about your emotions is weak.

However, what I have found is that the majority of people who say these kinds of things or believe this about mental health have either had no experience of it and simply don't understand, or they have lost someone to suicide and they think that it was just selfish and they are bitter about it.

I think that these words need to change. People acting like this are not attention-seeking, but help-seeking. If someone is willing to play with life and death then they do not want attention, they want help. That is what people who are struggling with mental-health issues and suicidal tendencies need: help.

I genuinely believe that if I had received proper early intervention, I could have been saved from years of struggling with these destructive thoughts, patterns and behaviours.

If people are 'acting out', behaving in extreme ways to try to express what they are feeling, what are you going to do? Are you going to show them the love and consistency that they are needing? Or shove them aside, thinking 'She'll be right'? When people act out it is usually a defence mechanism, a coping strategy designed to make them feel safer or more in control. Researchers have discovered that people do this when they are overwhelmed—they get an impulse to try to do something that expresses these strong emotions.

Almost every young person who has struggled with suicidal tendencies has heard the term 'attention-seeking'. This is not a stigma that those struggling can change, but society can. We must

remember to look beyond the behaviour to the 'why'.

When people are suicidal and are struggling with their mind, they might do something extreme like run away from home. To many, this is just seen as 'acting out', but for the person struggling, it is an impulsive expression of them trying to come down off the high-intensity emotional rollercoaster they are currently on. It is so important that the people around them understand this and try to get them the help they need, rather than looking down on their behaviour or writing it off as 'just trying to get attention'.

I can pretty much guarantee you that almost every young person who has struggled with suicidal tendencies has heard the term 'attention-seeking' at least one time in their journey. This is not a stigma that those struggling can change, but you can—society can. We must remember to look beyond the behaviour to the 'why'.

Section Three

ENGAGE

CHAPTER TWENTY

The battle

Knowing what you need to fight is one thing, but actually putting practical steps into action and working out how to fight is a whole other thing. Once I knew that I had these destructive beliefs that affected not only my thoughts but my behaviour, and I had figured out the root cause of them, I also began to re-examine the definition of fighting. I did this because I realised that knowing what it meant to fight would only get me so far—I needed to know what fighting actually looked like in practice.

So, as I re-read the definition, one of the first things that caught my eye was the word 'engage'. 'To *engage* in a battle or war.' What did it mean to actually engage in the battle? What I had discovered was that while I had *been present* in the battle, I most definitely was not engaging in it. I was doing the same things, having the same responses and going around in the same circles, over and over again. I had been repeating the same process for years, and every few months it would land me in hospital.

My process usually went like this: something would happen in my life (it could be something minor like someone not replying to a text message, or something major like severe bullying), I would begin to feel overwhelmed and my mind would go into battle mode. Waking up every single day thinking that no one could ever love you and that you are a burden to the world gets pretty draining, so at times it didn't take something huge to knock me over.

Knowing what it meant to fight would only get me so far—I needed to know what fighting actually looked like in practice.

I would begin to spiral downwards, usually very quickly. After a few hours of crying, listening to sad music and angry writing I would grab my pre-determined suicide method and run. Eventually, either when I was beginning the process of taking my life or fully unconscious and near death, the police would turn up. Sometimes they would find me because I had sent a goodbye message to someone saying where I was (I didn't always send out goodbyes, especially as I got older because I knew that person would potentially stop me) and other times because a member of the public had seen me and was concerned—they'd bike past me in the forest or see me from their window as I climbed to the edge of a cliff. I would be so angry that I'd failed again that I would fight with the police for a while, and then I would get taken to hospital.

When we got to hospital, if I was conscious I would get put into the Emergency Department, where I would sit in 'Room 6' (the white-walled, empty room they use for mental-health patients), with a police officer in the room and a security guard standing by the door. I would sit there for around six hours, while the understaffed mental-health crisis team did the rounds of every person in the hospitals around Auckland dealing with mental health (there are a lot of people struggling, and not enough workers). Then eventually two crisis-team workers would come into the room and assess me for about half an hour.

Thankfully, in 2019 the New Zealand government announced an entire restructure of the mental-health system and dedicated $1.9 billion towards funding it. This means there is now hope for change.

I got really good at learning what they wanted to hear, and could usually talk my way out of help pretty quickly. I'm not going to tell you what I would say (because I don't want to give anyone ideas on how to avoid mental-health services—these people are here to help, after all!) but the reason that I would do this was because at that stage I genuinely thought that nothing and no one could help me. I hated talking to mental-health workers because I felt like they were just 'being paid to care', and because I felt like it was totally pointless even trying to get help because I knew that I would just get put on a waiting list.

I didn't always respond like this, though; it became a learnt response from my earlier attempts. After I had moved to Auckland, on my fourth suicide attempt, I broke down when asked the question 'Do you still want to kill yourself?' and said yes. I told the mental-health worker that I still actively wanted to die and was going to try again—yet a couple of hours later they let me go home and told me a crisis-team worker would call me the next day to 'check in'! To me, that response confirmed my belief that they thought I was just an attention-seeker. Even if I told them I was still really battling in my mind they would just let me go anyway, so what was the point? So I learnt how to say what they wanted me to say, so they could clear me and get me out of the hospital bed (way to make a girl feel like a burden!).

Usually I was convincing enough to be let go, and the cycle would begin again a few weeks or months later. However, on my last few attempts they realised how intent I really was on dying and they started admitting me to the psych ward rather than letting me loose.

This process was different if I was brought in unconscious or comatose. In that case I would get taken straight to the Intensive Care I ward for medical treatment, but the end result was always the same—I would get moved down to a medical ward, where they would assess me and either let me go home or move me to the psych ward, where I would refuse help and eventually go back to my usual way of life.

At that stage I didn't want help and, in all honesty, the help I would have got was always pretty hit or miss anyway. Our mental-health system here in New Zealand is extremely broken, and from what I now know it's pretty similar worldwide. I never got the opportunity to do group therapy, or something helpful like cognitive or dialectical behavioural therapy (CBT or DBT), or acceptance and commitment therapy (ACT), because I was always on a waiting list. However, with the release of the new Wellbeing Budget, I am hopeful for change.

Also, I could not tell you the number of times that I have been in hospital with other young people with serious mental-health issues who had been told to 'come back when you have tried to kill yourself'. These people, who were clearly suicidal, were 'competing with' those who were acutely unwell with schizophrenic or other serious conditions for one of 20 beds in the mental-health ward. The funding and resources were just not there for enough people struggling with their mental health, and the system became overloaded to the point where people like myself were falling through the cracks, going months without the help we needed.

Thankfully, in 2019 the New Zealand government announced an entire restructure of the mental-health system and dedicated $1.9 billion towards funding it. This means there is now hope for change, but when I was in the system it was the total opposite.

Every time I tried to take my life, I really believed that this could be it. I didn't want to live anymore and I couldn't see any other way out. And every time that I failed I had the same horrible feeling of thinking that everyone hated me, that I was an inconvenience to all of these professionals and it would have been better if I had died. All of these thoughts and feelings would build up again and it wouldn't be long before I was acting on them, once again, trying to either hurt myself or take my life.

For some of you reading this book, this process will be all too familiar; to others, it will be beyond comprehension. But either way, my story stands as proof that it is possible to break a cycle that is this damaged, when you learn what engaging looks like and put it into action.

CHAPTER TWENTY-ONE

Phases of battle

A few weeks after the big conversation with Esther that we started this story with, I remember spending a whole day trying to figure out what it actually meant to fight, to work out how I could overcome the dark battle going on in my mind. While doing so, I came across an article about the process of soldiers going into war. I realised that while the situations were different, the fundamentals of an army battle could transfer to the battle of mental health. This is what I discovered:

PHASES OF AN ARMY BATTLE:

1. **Prepare**—intelligence-gathering phase.

In army terms, this is all about gathering information on the opponent and the battle that is about to take place. Who were they fighting? What were they fighting for? What are their opponent's strengths and weaknesses?

In my own case, when gathering intelligence and deciding what it was I was trying to fight, it was important not to confuse the *symptoms* of the problem with the underlying problem itself.

The underlying problem was not my suicidal behaviour—that was just a symptom. I had to fight the beliefs that put me in that state.

The underlying problem was not my suicidal behaviour—that was just a symptom. I didn't have to fight my suicidal tendencies, I had to fight the beliefs that put me in that state. This realisation was what kick-started that core-beliefs list I wrote.

While writing that list I began to untangle another belief, one that told me that my issue was just simply who I was. However, I now knew my illness was not my identity. And if this was not my identity, then maybe I wasn't fighting against myself, but against incorrect beliefs, behaviours and responses.

This is one of the key things to remember when it comes to engaging in the battle—you have to sit down and figure out what it is you are really fighting.

The 'intelligence-gathering' phase for this looks different for everyone, but I found a good place to start was finding stories of people who had overcome the same situations—researching what they learnt, how they got through. For me this meant spending hours finding stories of other people who had fought through mental illness, rather than spending hours binge-watching Netflix! I would literally google 'how to fight' and list all the practical things I could do, thinking about what had been stopping me from fighting and how I could push forward. I would read articles on websites like themighty.com and watch documentaries on YouTube about people who had survived mental illness and come out on top.

Don't mistake this phase for researching your illness, as sometimes this can do more harm than good. I know that for me when I was at one stage diagnosed with Borderline

Personality Disorder (BPD) I googled a bunch of stuff and read that there was no cure! This led me to me thinking 'Well then, there is no point because this is what I will be like forever'—which obviously was neither true nor helpful! (There are good evidence-based therapies for BPD!) This goes for all kinds of mental illness, though—if you start researching too deep into it you can begin to box yourself in and limit your thinking. Instead, this research is all about how you can fight your thoughts, behaviours and responses. What are the practical things that you can do to begin to engage in the battle?

2.	**Conduct**—initial (combat assault) phase. Also known as the 'action phase'.

For an army, this phase is the battle itself. The soldiers now know what they are fighting and how to best fight it and now it is time to do the work. It is all well and good to plan, think and talk about change, but the reality is that nothing will change until you actually action that change.

To be honest, I think that I did only the 'prepare and research' phase for so long. I would spend hours talking about change and complaining that nothing was happening, but I don't think I ever actioned the things I was saying. It would be like saying 'One day I am going to be a sports star' but then never getting on the field to practise. You can't think yourself to freedom, you have to action it.

For me personally, 'conduct' looked like a few different things. This is where I started to write those core-belief lists, where I started to engage in therapy for the first time (I will talk about this soon) and when I started to wake up every day choosing to engage in this battle and fight back for my life.

This wasn't easy. I couldn't tell you how many times I just wanted to quit and go back to my old ways, how many times I would be sitting there tempted to just run away again and hurt myself. I had to start using all of these urges as decision points to engage and put into practice the things I had to do to fight. I had to allow the people around me to support me, and I had to learn to trust that they wouldn't leave me if I told them the reality of what was going on for me. This meant actually having to reach out when things first came up and not waiting to hit tipping point before I called.

It is so important that we learn how to engage in this battle for our freedom—because once we gear up and begin to really fight, change may be closer than we think.

The people around me were incredible. They supported me with a lot of tough love (the kind of love that would say 'OK, Jazz, I'm so glad you reached out—it's horrible that you are feeling this way, but you know what you need to do to get yourself out of this'). This is important, because once they knew that I had been learning to fight, they knew that I could get through this, and they empowered me to do so. They didn't dive in and save me every time; instead, they encouraged me to do the work and to put in place the things I knew I needed to. There were times when they would just embrace me, but a lot of the time they challenged me, not giving me the answers but instead making me find the answers with them walking by my side. **Retraining your brain to believe that you are worth it may seem like only repetitive words that don't mean a lot for a while, but eventually it will become truth. One day you will wake up and believe it as fact.**

This phase of the battle is vital for the final phase, which is the breakthrough phase.

3. **Breakthrough**—this phase occurs when the attacking force breaks or penetrates their opponent's defensive line, and rapidly exploits that gap.

Once you have gathered the intelligence, engaged in the conduct and begun to action your fight, this is when the breakthrough can occur. Retraining your brain to believe that you are worth it may seem like only repetitive words that don't mean a lot for a while, but eventually it will become truth and one day you will wake up and believe it as fact; it will become a new belief. This isn't something that happens overnight, but with consistency and reworking your brain patterns you will start to see the difference.

I remember a key moment when I realised that my beliefs were changing; it was a very small but significant thing. I was at church one morning, and Wayne and Libby had been packing stuff out after the service. I was standing in the corridor backstage about to leave and Wayne and Libby both walked past me (they were in work mode!). Usually my mind would have freaked out at that point and I would have wondered what I did wrong and why they didn't say goodbye—but this time I didn't. This time I felt fully secure that they were just busy, and them not saying bye had absolutely nothing to do with my worth or their love for me. The months of hard work and core-belief contradiction writing had started to really pay off. I no longer second-guessed my worth based on their response, because I knew for a fact that they loved me.

Engaging in a battle is hard, because often we want to be able to jump straight through to the breakthrough phase. We want to just start living without this illness. But the reality is that it is a process—a process that can feel impossible (trust me, I know how that feels!). I could not tell you how many times I thought to myself that there was no point in trying to change things, or how many times I have heard other people say it. But it is so important that we learn how to engage in this battle for our freedom, despite everything in our life that tells us otherwise—because once we gear up and begin to really fight, change may be closer than we think.

CHAPTER TWENTY-TWO

Failure to engage

On reflection, I can understand why I struggled to engage in the battle for such a long time. My reality was that I believed that my illness had become part of my identity, and therefore it would never change. To my mind, I was depressed, I was broken, I was suicidal. These were not just things I was struggling with—they formed my personality and who I was.

Looking at it from a wider lens, I actually think a lot of this has to do with the way that we label mental illness. 'You are depressed', 'You are anorexic', 'You are Borderline'. You don't turn around to someone with cancer and say 'You are cancer', or to someone who has migraines and say 'You are a headache'. Is it any wonder that people who are experiencing mental illness struggle to understand the difference between this issue they are up against and who they are as a person?

If you are told enough times that you *are* something, eventually you will start to believe that, which was the case for me. From a young age I was told that I was just an attention-seeker and that I was Borderline. (Surprise—as I mentioned, I was diagnosed with Borderline Personality Disorder for a while. However, a couple of years later doctors decided that my behaviour and responses were actually a mix of posttraumatic stress disorder, anxiety and depression.) I was told I was depressed and that I was (and I quote) 'a lost cause'. Is it any wonder that as I got older, I believed that I could never separate myself from these things?

'You are depressed.' 'You are suicidal.' Is it any wonder that people who are experiencing mental illness struggle to understand the difference between this issue they are up against and who they are as a person?

I would never engage in therapy because I would walk in thinking, 'This is just who I am, so what is the point in trying?' I would refuse to take medication because I didn't think it would do anything to change me. I just accepted my suicidal thoughts, behaviours and feelings as a normal part of me.

If we want to enable people to start fighting before such warped beliefs are utterly ingrained in their minds, I believe that we really need to change the language around mental health—from 'You are anorexic' to 'You are struggling with anorexia', and from 'You are depressed' to 'You are struggling with depression'. If we can disassociate the illness from the person's identity and instead present it as something separate from who they are and something they are simply struggling with, hopefully it will mean that people will feel there is a point in trying to fight.

I was admitted into hospital countless times when I was struggling, and with 14 suicide attempts under my belt it was pretty obvious that I wasn't engaging. So many times I was told by nurses that I was wasting their time, that this was just who I was and I needed to stop burdening the hospital. I was also told I was a waste of space, I was attention-seeking or I wasn't worth helping because I wouldn't get better.

It is sad to think about the reality of the words people once spoke to me. Is it any wonder that time and time again I would sit in a hospital bed, surrounded by white walls, refusing to talk to the psych team? Why at times I would just say what they needed to hear and refused to engage in the things that they tried to offer me? If this was who I was and even the professionals thought so, then I wasn't going to try to engage in anything. Looking back, I see that during this time there were also people who spoke words of hope or love to me, but my beliefs about myself made it hard to see this and take them on board, and they were easily drowned out by negative words from others around me (particularly from those who were supposed to be in a caring role).

To be honest, I also think that I feared trying something new because what if it didn't work? What if I gave my everything to this new thing and I ended up finding out that this really *was* just who I am? To those who have not battled mental illness this can be confusing, but it is extremely common to think this way.

*

It was a bit like what I found out about myself a couple of years ago when I graduated from my course on Factual TV Directing at the South Seas Film & Television School, and I didn't tell anyone that there was a ceremony. My friends only found out about it after I posted a photo on social media of me walking across the stage.

I remember graduation and the lead-up to it so well. The school had announced that everyone had access to a few tickets for the graduation event, and I saw everyone else in my class going up and booking their tickets. I listened as everyone talked about who was coming, and heard stories of families travelling from overseas to be there. But I didn't tell anyone.

We need to change the language around mental health. If we can

disassociate the illness from the person's identity and instead present it as something they are simply struggling with, hopefully it will mean that people will feel there is a point in trying to fight.

In all honesty, this graduation was a big deal for me. It had been a huge and successful year. The course had launched me into the film industry, after my tutors had put me forward to pitch at the annual industry Doc Edge pitching forum (more on this later). The forum was usually only for experienced filmmakers, where they could pitch their ideas to broadcasters, funders and producers. However, they decided to accept my tutors' recommendation and I ended up winning the entire thing, the youngest director ever to do so. Because of this, I then left the course to start working on the series I had pitched. This meant that I didn't actually finish the directing course, but they decided they would still let me graduate because I was going to be learning more in the 'real world' than I would have in film school.

Despite this achievement, and despite the fact that my friends, including Wayne, Libby and Esther had been extremely supportive through the entire course, I still didn't tell them about the graduation ceremony. I wrote about six different messages to try to casually ask them if they wanted to come, but the fear of them saying no—or feeling like they had to come—overrode my deep desire to have them there. I ended up not telling anyone and going through the whole graduation day alone. And to be honest, it sucked. I watched everyone else with friends and family there, but for some reason I believed that the feeling of graduating alone was better than the feeling of being told that people didn't want to celebrate with me.

When she found out about this, Esther began asking me why I hadn't told anyone. I kind of just went around in circles saying that I didn't know why, and that it wasn't that important. Then she linked it to the subject of birthdays. You see, I was notorious for planning birthday celebrations and then cancelling them, like, a week out. I never really took time to think about why I did that, but in this conversation Esther said, 'Jazz, I think you have a fear of being celebrated.'

I sat there staring at her, feeling as if I had just been completely exposed. However, as I thought about it more I began to realise that I didn't have a fear of being celebrated—I had a fear of feeling rejected. Things like graduations or birthdays were an opportunity for people to hurt me, and so I would rather just not do anything than risk potentially being hurt.

I *wanted* to be celebrated. I wanted my friends around me to look back on what had been an incredible year, but I wasn't willing to risk rejection for celebration.

This was the same for birthdays. I have never in my life made a plan to celebrate my birthday and stuck to it. But it was not because I don't want to be celebrated, but the same thing—I feared rejection.

Turns out getting over that fear was a long process ... considering this graduation was only three years ago! It wasn't a fear that I was actively aware of, or maybe I just hadn't admitted it. But then I had to go through the same process that I did in breaking all of my other fears and go against my natural feelings to tell people when exciting things were happening in my life.

However, you will be happy to know that now I love celebrating and being celebrated! The first time I felt this way was in 2018, when Wayne and Libby put on a family dinner for my birthday. It was something we had started doing for everyone's birthday who was in the 'extended adopted family'. (Wayne and Libby are parent-figures to quite a few people, so there are about an extra eight people to their family of four!) At each birthday dinner they have started a tradition where they go around the table and everyone says one thing that they love about the birthday person.

I no longer fear being celebrated or fear those closest to me rejecting me, because their love and consistency over the years has taught me otherwise.

On my birthday, I remember looking around the table as we ate dinner and being so incredibly happy and thankful. Then they went around the table with everyone saying one thing they loved about me and I cried, laughed and felt so incredibly loved. It was the first birthday that I hadn't despised or spent waiting for the day to end.

I'm not going to lie—it was a fight to actually get me to their house in the first place, but once I got there I was so glad that I did! Now we do this every year, and I no longer fear being celebrated or fear those closest to me rejecting me, because their love and consistency over the years has taught me otherwise.

When I think about mental illness and my personal inability to engage in the battle, it was never about not wanting to be free of my thoughts and behaviours, but all about the 'what if?'—the same kind of 'what if' that made me cancel every birthday celebration. Instead of the fear of failure, it was fear of being reminded that this was simply who I was.

If I took a risk and asked people to celebrate my birthday and they didn't want to or didn't turn up, then my mind would tell me that I really was unlovable—just like my thoughts had been telling me. It was similar when it came to engaging in the battle. What if I gave my everything to it and it didn't work? If it didn't work, that would mean I really was a lost cause and that I was all of the things my mind had been telling me.

That fear can be powerful, and it was only once I learnt to overcome it that I could truly say I was engaging in the battle.

CHAPTER TWENTY-THREE

Behind the fear

Looking back, I can see many times when I refused to engage out of fear and out of a certainty that this was just who I was and it couldn't be changed. One time in particular stands out to me.

When I was 16 and made the decision to move to Auckland, I ended up in some pretty awful situations. As you read earlier, I moved from house to house and also lived in women's refuges, motels and hotels. I also went to two different high schools.

One day when I was sitting in my dance class at my new school, I got tagged in something on Facebook. Someone had made a page called 'Jazz Thornton is an attention-seeking slut'.

I saw the page and ran out of the dance room, locking myself in the bathrooms close by. I read through the comments with tears streaming down my face. 'She deserves to die', 'She should just kill herself', 'Can't she see that everyone hates her?' At this stage the kids at this new school hadn't been bullying me—they didn't really know too much about me, as I had only been there for about two months. The page was set up by someone in my hometown of Timaru, but had got to the kids at my new school because I was getting tagged in stuff on the page, meaning it was coming up on everybody's news feed.

I felt my self-hatred rising, so I grabbed my bag and tried to run out of school. One of my teachers caught me and sat me down in her office. She knew about the page because other kids in the school had seen it and were all talking about it. I pulled out my phone and showed her the page and all of the comments. As I sat there scrolling through them, I felt my heart shattering. The teacher ended up keeping me in the office until about 5p.m., well after school hours, when she finally felt that it was safe enough to let me go because I seemed to have calmed down somewhat. She arranged for one of my friends from school to drive me home. (At this stage I still had some good friends at this new school, and to be honest that was probably because I was still new and nobody knew my history.)

He dropped me home and said that he was going to call me later that night, and that if I didn't answer he was going to call the police. I just smiled and got out of the car.

I ran inside and up to my bedroom, grabbed a few things and then ran straight back out of the house. Jumping on a bus, I decided to go as far away from where I was living as possible.

As I was on the bus I looked at the page again, reading all of the comments from people in my hometown and now also people at my new school who had jumped on after word got around. It felt like the entire world hated me and that it made sense for me to just die, because what was the point in being alive?

When the bus finally got to its last stop I jumped off and ran to a nearby bush area. I threw my phone a few metres away from me and began the process of taking my life, sitting there overdosing as I cried.

What I didn't realise was that the friends I had made at this new school had been trying to call me, and they had now called the police. There was an active search underway for me, but I had no idea.

It wasn't long before police were able to work out where I was. I began to see the beams of flashlights coming towards me. A female officer and her male partner pulled me up off the ground and out of the bush area I was in and laid me on the concrete path, where I started to dip in and out of consciousness.

One of the most important lessons I learnt was to let mental-health professionals do their job and trust that they know what they are doing.

A few hours later when I woke up in the hospital, I was fuming. I did not want to wake up this time—how did everyone not see that I was better off gone? How did they not understand that I was a burden to everyone around me and that I was all of the things the bullies had been saying online?

I refused to talk to the nurses and doctors, turning my face away and curling up in a ball. When the psych team eventually came in, I decided to throw on a face that would get me out of the hospital because I didn't want their help. I didn't want to be alive and I didn't want to be back in the mental-health system again. I pretended I was fine, and as one of the team sat there asking me if I would do group therapy or if I would allow them to put me in touch with a bunch of different services, I refused. In my mind I was thinking 'I am not even going to give these things a try or engage in them, because it is pointless. This is who I am. No one can help me.'

Looking back at that moment, I realise now that if I had chosen to give it a go and engage despite my fears, I could have saved myself years of struggle. I mean, after all, these professionals probably do know what they are doing a lot more than me!

*

As I discovered this fear that I had of engaging, I began to look back to where it might have come from. But I found there wasn't one incident that I can pinpoint as 'the moment it all went south'. Instead, I can see a multitude of situations that developed these fears.

By the time I was nine years old I had already moved schools three times. One day in particular I was out playing basketball with my class in PE. A kid threw me the ball and when I caught it, my thumb got pulled back so far it pretty much touched my forearm. I had a tendency to be dramatic, but I was in excruciating pain. I got taken up to the school sick bay. As I was sitting there crying, a teacher walked in. He began talking to the reception staff and I heard him say, 'Don't worry, this is Jazz we are talking about. This is just who she is. She is just being dramatic.'

Sitting on the small, cold bed in the sick bay, everything inside of me shrivelled up. I suddenly wanted to hide my pain, pretend it wasn't there. I also remember playing his words 'this is just who she is' over and over again in my head. This was my teacher, a man who I looked up to, who I adored and thought the world of. A man who in just one sentence, not recognising the vulnerable space I was in, especially at such a young age, reinforced the belief that this was just 'who I am', and that I needed to put up guards to keep myself safe. That was one of the first times I had heard first-hand that this was just who I was, and I don't think I or my teacher had any idea the impact that would go on to have. (By the way, he might have thought I was faking being hurt, but my mum took me to the hospital after school and they X-rayed it and found a small hairline fracture, so the next day I walked into the school with a cast on my hand.)

I think that another reason I struggled to engage was a really bad experience I had with a counsellor. This counsellor really didn't like me, and she went out of her way to make it known. She had previously said to my face that I caused too many issues and she would always make 'ugh' kind of sounds whenever I was talking to her. She told me that I was always the centre of drama and I needed to get over it, because other kids needed her help more than I did.

One day I went to see her after I had broken down to my teacher about the bullies at school. She sat me down, saying that I was an attention-seeker, that I would never amount to anything, and that I was a lost cause. This was a woman who was supposed to be trained to help me.

But once I made the decision (and when I say decision, I mean decision after decision after decision) to engage despite the fears, everything began to change.

I never did any proper counselling with her. I tried a few times but quickly discovered that she wasn't helpful. Having my trust in her broken and my heart shattered by her words, I can understand why I didn't want to engage in therapy for so many years after this.

Young people who have had traumatic experiences or hold beliefs like the ones that I once held really struggle to comprehend professional help. They throw up barriers and often refuse to listen to anything counsellors or other support people have to say, because they believe that the professional only seems to care because that is their job. So many young people have said to me, 'They are just paid to care.' However, being in the position that I am now in and having many friends who are counsellors, I have discovered how much they actually *do* care. Trust me, none of them get into it because of the money! Yes, it is their job, but they do their job *because they care.*

Just like an artist creates art because they enjoy it, or a scientist chooses to spend hours in a lab trying to solve a problem—they get into it because they care about it, because they are passionate about it. The same applies for professionals in mental health. One of the most important lessons I learnt was to let them do their job and trust that they know what they are doing.

There were many reasons that I thought I couldn't engage, many fears and responses that prevented me from engaging, often without me even realising that was what was happening. But once I made the decision (and when I say decision, I mean decision after decision after decision) to engage despite the fears, everything began to change.

CHAPTER TWENTY-FOUR

Breakthrough

Looking back, I remember the first time in my life that I started to realise that maybe my struggles and mental illness were not my identity. I was at my doctor's—on the surface talking to her about a medical problem, but really hoping to get the final amount of pills I needed to complete an overdose.

At this point in my life I had recently come back from Australia after trying to run away, and had got a new job working as a receptionist. I aced the interview and was really good at the job, so much so that they let me sign a full-time contract before my trial period was over. However, it wasn't too long before my mental-health issues ramped up again, and while I tried to not let it leak into my work life, it did start to affect it when I had to take a couple of days off after being hospitalised for hurting myself.

When the manager found out why I was in hospital she called me and said that it would be best that I didn't come back into work. They knew they couldn't legally fire me and so instead she asked me (i.e. told me) to resign.

Thinking back, I never actually resigned, so I know for a fact that what that company did wasn't legal, but more so, it took away the very last thing keeping me alive. Having a job and responsibility gave me a sense of self-worth and got me out of the house every day. When that was suddenly taken away from me I totally spiralled down.

My GP, Dr Stephanie Taylor, could tell that I really wasn't doing OK. At the time I didn't think anyone could tell what was going on inside my head, but I recently asked her about it and she said that while I was verbally saying I was OK, I refused to look up at her and my entire body language was screaming that I was really struggling. She knew my history, too, so she began to ask me questions like 'How are you really doing?' and 'What are the thoughts you are having at the moment?', so she could try to figure out what was really going on.

I decided to engage, to fill my diaries with ways I could fight, and started choosing to try to believe what those who loved me said over what my mind was telling me.

I was really stubborn at the start, refusing to talk about it. I had no intention of engaging in the conversation. What was supposed to be a 15-minute appointment turned into over an hour and a half. We went back and forth, with Dr Stephanie trying to get me to tell her where I was really at, and me being too scared to tell her. I didn't want her to know how broken I really was.

Eventually, as she continued to persist, I began to feel like maybe she did actually care. Tears started rolling down my cheeks as she began to tell me that my life was worth it, that *I* was worth it. Dr Stephanie kept talking, saying that she truly believed that I could live without this pain and without this constant mental battle. This was the first time that I had ever been told by a professional that maybe my mental illness and pain wasn't who I was—that it wasn't something that I just had to 'learn to manage' but that it was something that one day I could possibly live without. If a doctor believed that I could actually live a happy life, then maybe there was something worth fighting for?

I broke down and told her that I had been stockpiling medication. I had an entire drawer filled with all kinds of methods, and I had planned to use them later that night.

Dr Stephanie grew increasingly concerned for me and organised for the police to go to my house and clear my room. As she did this, I sat in her office screaming, crying and repeatedly saying, 'Please just let me die!' My mind was going a million miles an hour. Those things were my security, my backup plan. They were the thing that meant I had control of when I could end it all. **If a doctor believed that I could actually live a happy life, then maybe there was something worth fighting for?**

For anyone I know who has been suicidal, feeling like this is common.

This is why when counsellors create safety plans for people who are suicidal, the first priority is usually elimination of method. This basically means getting rid of anything in your reach or possession that you could hurt yourself with, or take your life with. Safety plans also involve working out who to contact when you are feeling at risk, and methods you can use to help calm yourself down. Dr Stephanie was eliminating the suicide method that I had planned for a long time, and it broke me. I was in uncontrollable tears, knees pulled up towards my chest and pulling away as she tried to console me.

'My mind is telling me to run and give up right now but she inserted a tiny voice in the back of my mind saying "keep trying". So I will...'

Eventually I pulled my gaze up to hers and gave in to her persistent suggestion of taking me to the hospital so that I could get properly assessed by the mental-health team and admitted into the psych ward. I now know that if I hadn't agreed to go, she would have put me in hospital under the

Mental Health Act and made me go anyway ... this way was just a lot nicer, with me agreeing to it. This is called being 'sectioned', and in New Zealand it means that you are legally required to stay at the psych ward for at least five days and comply with treatment. You are not allowed to leave during this time, and you are assessed most days by the clinical team. After five days they can extend it out to 14 or 21 days, and then after that the section goes before a judge to sign off if you need to stay there for a longer term. I knew if I went voluntarily, I had much more control over how long I spent in hospital and what treatment I could undertake.

This turned out to be the final time that I had an active suicide plan, and the final time I got admitted into the psych ward. Looking back, I realise that the persistence of my doctor (whose job was only to see me for 15 minutes for a medical issue) was the first turning point that enabled me to engage in this battle. I found a diary entry from the day after this encounter, which explains the impact that day had in emotional detail:

I don't know how I ended up here again. I feel so incredibly broken and like the entire world looks at me like they want me gone. I am so over all of this pain, and waking up every single day of my life wishing I was someone else. Wishing I was never born.

I am sitting in hospital again and I am so angry because this time I was so sure that my plan was going to work. I had everything set up but just needed more pills to ensure I could do the job properly. My doctor clicked onto it though and she realised that I wasn't okay.

I don't understand why she cares. She kept saying that I have a future and that one day I will look back at an incredible life that I could make for myself. She is a doctor and she knows my history, I don't understand. I don't understand why she spent so much time with me and why she didn't just let me go. She didn't have to sit with me for over an hour but she did.

I can't help but wonder if maybe she can see something that I can't? I don't know why, but hearing a doctor say that there is hope for me has made me think that maybe, just maybe, there is. That maybe I can get through this? I don't know. It is pretty overwhelming at the moment. But I am going to try really hard to prove her right. My mind is telling me to run and give up right now but she inserted a tiny voice in the back of my mind saying 'keep trying'. So I will. For now anyway . . .

It was after this hospital admission that I really decided to stop surviving and start fighting. It was once I was released from several months in the psych ward that I had that life-changing conversation with Esther that started this book; when I decided to engage; when I started to fill my diaries with ways I could fight; and started choosing to believe what those who loved me said over what my mind was telling me.

This journey would be long and hard, mainly because while I was learning to fight I had to battle with my thoughts every single day. I had to learn to trust those around me, trust that they wouldn't leave me and trust that their words were true. The battle for my life was in full force. It was time to really engage.

CHAPTER TWENTY-FIVE

'Dear Suicidal Me'

One of the biggest and probably most significant things that I did to engage was writing a letter that started 'Dear Suicidal Me'. Psychologists often create safety plans for people who are struggling with mental-health issues and suicidal thoughts, which are great, but it is a whole other thing when the plan comes from yourself. I knew my pattern—I knew that I would end up trying to take my life again very soon, and so when I had a slightly good day, I wrote this:

Dear Suicidal Me,

If you are reading this, then I am guessing things aren't going too well for you. I know that it probably seems impossible, that you have gone around in another circle and that it would be better with you gone. You think you are a burden to everyone around you and that no one could possibly love you — but you are wrong. There are people who love you.

You know what you need to do to bring yourself back up from this space. Put on inspirational music (not sad music like you always do, you know this makes you feel worse yet you still choose to do it). Text Esther, Libby or Wayne — remember, you are not alone and people care, so please get over your pride and fear and reach out. They would rather have you messy and alive than not here at all.

You are so close to being free of this all, don't give up now ... Remember who and what you are fighting for, people DO care about you and you have a future. It's not about battling your past but fighting for that future. Start fighting right now, take those steps ...

You've got this.

Jazz

This letter was something that I pulled out countless times following my discharge from the psych ward. Every time that I felt like I wanted to give up I would read it and remind myself of how to fight, who I was fighting for and what I was fighting for.

When you are in high crisis and your thoughts are running a million miles an hour, it is so difficult to remember the people who care about you. It is difficult to remember the practical things you can do to help bring yourself down from this place, and it is pretty much impossible to think about any future plans that you have. This letter had all of the above in it, so when it came down to these moments of being overwhelmed, it helped bring me back down to reality and be reminded of what I needed to do to fight.

Medication isn't for everyone, but it can be used as a tool to help your brain even out a bit while you learn how to fight.

I could never have imagined at this stage that one day I would take this letter with me to film school, and create the very first viral video for Voices of Hope out of it. This letter didn't only save my life—it changed it completely.

Every time I was admitted to hospital, I was always put on different antidepressant and anti-anxiety medications. Some of them did not work at all and felt like they took away my entire personality, but when I eventually found something that worked (and I took it consistently), I found that it levelled me out enough for me to be able to learn how to engage and how to fight. It is really hard to fight when you are just up and down all the time, so finding an antidepressant that helped level me out a little enabled me to engage more than I could when I was off medication (or on the wrong meds).

Medication isn't for everyone, but it can be used as a tool to help your brain even out a bit while you learn how to fight. What works for one person in regards to medication won't necessarily work for another, but in order for it to do its job you have to take it consistently.

One of the other huge steps that I took in actively fighting was the decision to actually engage in therapy. Don't get me wrong—I had been going to therapy on and off for years, but the longest I had ever seen the same person was about three sessions. I never got immediate help after my hospital admissions because the waiting lists were so long to get therapy, and when I would eventually get seen by the clinical care team I would just convince them I was fine and would be discharged from the system.

I didn't like people getting to know the real me, and also, as I have said earlier, I didn't see the point in going. I would walk into the appointments with the attitude of 'this is part of my identity therefore it will never change, so what is the point in even trying?' I also think that part of this came from a broken trust of professionals after being let down as a little girl when I was being abused.

Once I decided to go in with that mindset of engaging and just giving everything a go, I started to see true change.

One day I decided that I needed to try to see a psychologist again. I had very little trust in them, so this time I wanted to find one who I could really relate to. Because I had been sexually abused as a child, I was able to access free therapy through ACC (this applies no matter how historic the abuse is, and the majority of counsellors and therapists in New Zealand are ACC registered). I sat down one night and began scrolling through a list of psychologists on the ACC website and came across one called Sara. I thought I'd give her a try.

I remember telling her straight up at our very first appointment that I didn't like or trust psychologists, and that I hadn't seen anyone for longer than three sessions. Sara laughed, and we decided to make it a goal for me to try to see her for at least four sessions.

'Remember who and what you are fighting for, people DO care about you and you have a future. It's not about battling your past but fighting for that future. Start fighting right now.'

Those four sessions turned into over a year of ongoing therapy. It took time, but as I began to go into the sessions with the thought that 'if I engage and do the things she tells me to do, then maybe things will get better', a lot of my mental obstacles were forced down and I learnt how to engage.

It took a lot of time to build up trust with her, but she saw that I was afraid and so she let me choose where each session went. How far into detail we talked about things and the topics and events we discussed were fully up to me.

At the start I kept it all pretty super-ficial—surface-level stuff—but then eventually she would ask me questions that would help lean the conversation towards the real issues I was facing. The beliefs, behaviours and patterns that had been formed as part of my past slowly started to come out into the open. As hard as it was, what I found was that actually talking about these things in a safe place helped remove the shame of them and allowed me to start to see them as something separate from who I was. Investing the time into actually untangling all of the lies and warped beliefs that had been built up in my brain was difficult, but when I found the right therapist it became one of the most vital parts of my recovery, and my life did begin to change.

One of the other reasons that I had hated seeing therapists was because of that belief I mentioned above—'They are just being paid to care, they don't actually care.' However, the more I saw Sara, the more I began to realise that wasn't true. She was in this job because she *did* care, she believed in me and she genuinely thought that one day I could get better.

Learning to trust the professionals around me and trust in their qualifications was a huge step for me. These people have studied the brain and how our minds work for years, and for me to walk in thinking that they didn't know anything halted my healing journey for such a long time.

*

Learning how to engage in all of these areas is what enabled me to really start fighting. It was learning how to engage that unlocked the kind of breakthrough that saw my beliefs break and re-form. Once I decided to go in with that mindset of engaging and just giving everything a go, I started to see true change.

I was engaging in the battle, but I knew the war was far from over. Engaging isn't something that you can only do once or twice and then see breakthrough—you need to choose to engage whenever you possibly can, and you are only able to do that through the power of your decisions.

CHAPTER TWENTY-SIX

Strengths

My breakthrough lay in my decisions. And I mean every single decision that I made when I decided to fight—decisions about when to ask for help, decisions to not run away when I wanted to, or decisions to pull out a pen and draw on paper instead of putting a blade to my skin.

I have always been a really quick thinker, and therefore I can also be really quick at making decisions. Today this is a great advantage and I view it as one of my strengths, but in the past it could make me impulsive, acting without thinking and overreacting to circumstances. It was one of the reasons I would spiral downwards so quickly and at times decide to try to take my life after only a few hours of being in crisis.

As part of my recovery, and while I was thinking about my core beliefs and how my mind could work against me, I was interested to find out more about my personality and how that contributed to my mental health—positively and negatively. In 2017 I did the Gallup StrengthsFinder test (now called CliftonStrengths), which is a world-renowned test that identifies the strengths of your personality type, so you can maximise them in your professional or personal life. I remember doing it once a few years earlier, when I was studying at Equippers College, but I couldn't remember my results so I decided to do it again.

It is an online test that takes about 30 minutes to complete, with you answering a bunch of questions that cover a range of topics and scenarios. It then analyses your responses, and sorts them into one of four domains, which describe how you use your strengths and talents to work with information, make things happen, influence others and build relationships (called Strategic Thinking, Executing, Influencing and Relationship Building). It then goes into detail about particular themes within those domains that you are strong in.

For people who are trying to improve their performance at work, for example, you can use this information to work out how to best utilise your strengths in an office environment. But for me it was interesting to see how these aspects of my personality had worked *against* me in the past, as well as how I could utilise them in my battle for freedom from mental illness.

The test identifies your top five strengths, but for me the top three really stood out as being relevant to my battle. They were:

- Futuristic (in the Strategic Thinking domain)
- Strategic (also Strategic Thinking)
- Woo (Influencing)

Luckily for me, Libby is a qualified strengths coach, so I went to see her to talk through my results. Meeting with a strengths coach helps you identify how your strengths operate in your life and how they work together.

I sat down with Libby and we started talking through my strengths. As we got talking, I began to realise that the things that were my biggest strengths also became my biggest weaknesses when I was unwell.

My top two strengths were both from the Strategic Thinking domain. I scored most highly in Futuristic, which means that I love to see, plan and work towards the future. I like to dream big. This is the strength that has enabled me to do all that I do now, why I have such big dreams and then go out and chase them. However, when I was struggling with mental illness, I struggled to see a future at all. Seeing as my top strength is Futuristic, no wonder I found that so hard! **Decision-making has been absolutely key in my recovery. Once I had decided to fight and use my decision-making skills for good, there was no stopping me.**

I remember being really surprised when I first saw this as my top strength, probably because it felt kind of ironic and strange that a girl who once wanted to die had Futuristic as her top strength. However, it also made total sense for where I was in 2017—I was through my illness, had huge dreams for the future and was always looking for 'where to next?'. But it also made total sense to me how this strength would operate as my biggest weakness when it wasn't being used.

I think in hindsight I have always been Futuristic, ever since I was a little kid, but the events in my life had turned the future into something terrifying for me. I felt like I had nothing to live for, nothing to work for and that the future was something I would never see.

Strategic was my second strength, also in the Strategic Thinking domain. This is another quality that I know I have always had. It allows me to be a really quick thinker, which in most environments is great. I was really good at studio directing when I was studying at film school, because if something went wrong I was able to quickly come up with a solution and execute it in a calm manner. This strength is also what helped me come up with all the campaigns and reach for my charity, Voices of Hope, as well as what enables me to perform in under-pressure situations like public speaking. It is the strength that ensures I can talk down people in high crisis. This strength means I can act fast and I often find solutions before other people.

However, this quick thinking also probably got me into the most trouble when I was unwell. It was the kind of thinking that meant I would take one innocuous statement and twist it to mean someone hated me. I was always over-analysing situations. Where I think it affected me the most, however, was my impulsive decision-making. Because of how fast I would think, I could have a suicidal thought and then in less than 15 minutes I was trying to take my life.

I remember one day like this really well. I was sitting at home watching TV and writing in my diary. I had felt fine that morning and everything had seemed pretty normal, but as I started writing I could literally see the transition from 'normal' writing to 'I hate myself so much—why am I like this?'. My quick-thinking brain grabbed onto this new train of thought and ran with it, sending me into a rapid spiral. I then became overwhelmed with suicidal thoughts.

I grabbed a suicide method that I had stashed and within about 15 minutes I was in the middle of a forest near my house, trying to take my life. I was determined to not wake up this time.

I remember going way off the path, ensuring that no one could see me. Thankfully, there was this one guy who was biking in the forest who decided to bike off-track. He found me just as I was becoming unconscious.

I don't remember being found—I just woke up in the Intensive Care Unit of the hospital. There were tubes everywhere and I was unable to breathe by myself, but I was alive. It was exactly like you see in the movies—waking up to a white room, staring at a white roof with white machines hovering above you. My hands were tied down to the bed to stop me from pulling out my breathing tube. As I lay there waking up, I thought to myself, 'How on earth did I get here?'.

This entire situation could have been prevented had I learnt earlier the destructive power of my quick decision-making. If I had chosen to sit with my feelings a little longer, knowing they would pass eventually, and not run to the forest, then I wouldn't be lying in a hospital bed fighting for my life.

That suicide attempt was the closest I had ever come to death, and it was pretty darn close. I was covered in tubes and wires and attached to monitors—all because of that one impulsive decision, I was now in an incredible amount of pain (anyone who has been awake with a full breathing tube down their throat knows what I am talking about—it is horrible).

I was so lucky to have survived it, and while at the time I didn't feel lucky, as I lay there I realised I needed to learn to stop thinking myself into a spiral, to reach out before getting to the crisis point.

The worst part about this entire situation is it happened during a time when I had pushed away Wayne, Libby and Esther. I had stopped talking to them, I wasn't going to church and my whole circle of friends had changed. I remember after the breathing tube got removed, the nurse asked me if I wanted the hospital to call Esther, as she was on my emergency contact list. I said no, I didn't want anyone to know. And so, nobody knew for weeks that I had been in a coma, that I had nearly died. All because of my decisions.

That was a moment when I could have chosen to accept help, to allow them to call her and let her back in. Instead, I made the decision to take the hard route of continuing to try to do this by myself, out of shame. I didn't want her to be disappointed in me or to have to face up to what I had done and that I was still in this cycle. This meant that the year leading up to my final suicide attempt was pretty lonely, because I continuously refused to reach out for help.

I began to realise that the things that were my biggest strengths also became my biggest weaknesses when I was unwell.

I would say that the majority of my suicide attempts were impulsive. I always had a plan for how I would take my life, and most of the time had a suicide note at hand, but I would always make the decision to act on my thoughts very spontaneously. As you can see, my quick thinking may have been my greatest strength, but it also played against me when used in a negative way.

As I have talked about before, this had me in continuous crisis, living in a way that no person was designed to live. I felt like I couldn't stop myself—that when the urge to hurt myself came I had to run with it, I had to give in to it. These impulsive decisions led to multiple suicide attempts and hospital admissions, windows being smashed by police to try and get to me, frequent self-harm, and constant lying to people. Learning how to control these impulses became key in enabling me to fight well, something I will go into detail about in the next chapter. As long as my thoughts and impulses ruled my life I wasn't going to get anywhere.

*

From the test I had done, there was one other strength that stood out for me, under the domain of Influencing. This was Woo, which related to my ability to connect quickly in an authentic way to win people over. When operating out of this strength, it means being able to work a room, drawing people into your vision and naturally stepping into roles of leadership, as people are drawn to you.

However, when I was in the depth of my illness, my Woo is what enabled me to talk myself out of many situations. It was the ability to sit and talk to a nurse, convincing her that I was OK enough to leave hospital when I wasn't. It meant I was able to talk my way out of counselling and enabled me to live a lot of my life without my friends knowing how much I was struggling.

It also meant that so much of my identity was based on what people thought of me. Woo is all about winning people over, but it also means that you are acutely aware of what people are thinking about you. You have the need to be liked, and for someone who believes that she is unlovable and a burden it felt like it was forever a losing battle.

The most detrimental side of this is that it meant that my mind believed what people said or thought was fact. If I felt someone thought I was annoying, then I took on the identity of annoying. If they were expressing that they thought that I was 'too much to handle', then I was too far gone.

It worked against me in so many ways, including when it came to receiving proper help from mental-health professionals, because my inner Woo would kick in and I would want them to like me. I never let them know what was really going on, the reality of the thoughts in my head or how I felt, because I wanted them to think I 'had it together' and that I was a strong fighter. This also kept all of my friendships at a surface level, wanting to ensure that people liked me but never really got to know me.

Learning how to use Woo as a strength is one of the biggest things that enabled me to do a lot of what I now do. It gives me the ability to stand up in front of huge crowds and win them over, to a point where they feel hope is real. It enables me to pitch, tell stories and get people behind my visions. The challenge for me was learning to overcome the belief that my identity lay in what people said about me, and instead, believing in who I actually was.

*

Learning about my strengths and how they could actually operate as weaknesses was interesting, but the most important thing to come out of the test was recognising my tendency to make quick decisions. Decision-making has been absolutely key in my recovery. Having very fast, impulsive reactions to things meant that every single decision I made mattered, good and bad. And once I had decided to fight and use my decision-making and strategic thinking skills for good, there was no stopping me.

CHAPTER TWENTY-SEVEN

The power of decisions

It wasn't until I did that test that I really thought about how aspects of my personality and my strengths could affect my mental health, through my reactions and approaches to things. Before this, I had never really thought about my impulsiveness and where it had come from—I assumed it had just been a part of me and how I was. For the most part, I think this is true. I have always been a quick thinker and in most situations that is a great thing, but as trauma intercepted my life it changed the way that I used this strategic side.

Reading my CYFS files, I can see that even from a young age I always had huge, out-of-proportion responses to events. One time I hit another kid and was found curled up, 'crying in the corner'. My response to something pretty minor (and that a lot of kids do) was extreme, and while I don't know why I acted this way, I do know that the abuse and manipulation I suffered as a three-year-old had a lot to do with it.

However, on the upside, the great thing is that I discovered that it was possible to restore that strength of Strategic to its original intention. I could use my decision-making to fight back rather than destroy myself.

Revolution Tour is a travelling road show that goes around New Zealand high schools, spreading a message of hope and positivity using music and dance. I remember when it came to my first high school, in Timaru—that's when I first met Esther. Since then I have had the privilege of touring with the group, too. One of the things the leaders often say to kids is, 'The decisions you make in life, make your life.'

This couldn't be more true for me. The decisions that I was making in my life were not decisions that developed a fight within me, but the kind of decisions that dug me deeper into a mess. It was possible for my world to change, but the change lay within my decisions: my decision to believe the people who said they loved me over what my mind told me (the opposite). The decision to call a friend instead of writing a suicide letter.

It was possible for my world to change, but the change lay within my decisions: my decision to believe the people who said they loved me over what my mind told me. The decision to call a friend instead of writing a suicide letter. All of these decisions are hard ones, but they enable you to engage in the fight, break distorted beliefs and allow you to begin healing.

The decision to be around people when all I wanted to do was isolate myself. All of these decisions are hard ones—trust me, I know—but they are the kinds of decisions that enable you to engage in the fight, break distorted beliefs and allow you to begin healing.

*

One of the decisions that changed everything for me was the one I made when I got out of the psych ward for the very last time (you read about how I ended up there in chapter 24). I had been in the ward for a couple of months, and by the time I got released it was four days before Christmas. After my release, I was told that someone from the crisis team would call me every single day to check in and see if I was OK.

On Christmas Eve I got that call. The lady on the phone asked me how I was doing and how I was feeling on a scale of 1 to 10 (a question that you get asked so many times when you are in the mental-health system). She then told me that this time of the year was when they lost the greatest number of people in my kind of situation. **Your life doesn't change based on the actions of others, but because of your own decisions. Your decisions have the ability to change everything.**

I hung up the phone and lay on the mattress on the floor of my room and just started crying. In that moment, something rose up inside me that said

'I don't want to be another statistic'. It was about 11p.m., and I spontaneously decided to get in a taxi and go to the Christmas Eve service that was on at Equippers.

I had stopped going to church regularly about a year before my final suicide attempt—I would try to go every now and then, but I found it too hard to turn up every week. During this time, people like Wayne, Libby and Esther were still trying to talk with me and encourage me every now and then, but I had pushed everyone close to me away, so deciding to go back was a huge thing for me. I remember I was filled with anxiety as I rang the taxi. I was so nervous to see everyone, wondering what they would think of me and what they would say about me—but part of me also knew that I had tried to do this by myself for long enough and it wasn't working. I needed to surround myself with people again.

I knew the church would be filled with people who knew me and had seen me fall so deeply over the last couple of years—people like Esther, Wayne and Libby, who I had run away from because they knew my darkest side. I was so certain that they all hated me. From a logical viewpoint, the people in the church had never said or acted in a way that suggested that they hated me, but because I knew what I had done and I hated myself, I viewed them through the lens that I viewed myself.

As the taxi pulled up outside the theatre where the service was being held, I got out and ran to the corner of the street. I stood there pretending to be on the phone, waiting for everyone to go inside because I didn't want anyone to see me or try to talk to me.

Once I knew the service had started, I walked inside and sat right at the back by myself. But before I knew it a woman named Peta came and sat next to me. I knew Peta from church but we had never really hung out or had a full conversation. I felt my heart start to beat a little faster as she sat there. I had wanted to try to get through the entire service unseen.

After the service Peta started to talk to me and asked what I was doing for Christmas Day. I didn't have any plans—in fact, I just wanted to sit in bed all day and isolate myself, because the holiday season was really hard for me, given my history. Before I knew it, Peta had invited me to spend Christmas with her family.

I was so confused about why she would do that, why she would care enough about someone she didn't really know to have them over for this special family day. It took some persuasion on her part, but in that moment I decided that now was another opportunity to fight. It was an opportunity to choose to not isolate myself and go against my natural instincts that would tell me to run away because I was going to be a burden to her family. I said yes, and she drove me to my house so I could get some things and come and stay the night.

The next morning we woke up bright and early on Christmas Day. I hadn't realised that Peta was rostered on to sing at the morning church service, meaning that we had to leave early and would be the first people there. This terrified me, because it meant that I couldn't just sneak in the back after everyone was inside—it meant that people would see me. I was so afraid of what they would think.

As we walked inside, our senior pastor, Kathy, was standing in the foyer. Immediately she came up to me and started talking to me and laughing with me, asking me my plans for the day and saying how great it was to see me. I was so confused. Once again, why was she talking to me? Why did she care?

I had to stop and think to myself: what are the consequences of this decision I am about to make? Does it get me closer to, or further away from, my future?

And in that moment I felt my belief of being a burden and being unlovable start to crack. If someone who knew how broken I was, knew of the things I had done and the shame I was carrying didn't hate me and welcomed me back with open arms, then maybe what my mind was telling me wasn't true? Looking back now, I see how that vital decision on Christmas Eve—to not be a statistic, and to walk back into a place where people knew me and loved me—was the start of my change. That one decision I made to not isolate myself enabled me to unlock something that taught me what unconditional love was.

When I saw Wayne and Libby walk in to the service, I went up to them and wrapped my arms around them both, breaking down into tears. I felt so thankful to know that they were still there for me. Despite everything, neither they nor Esther had ever given up on me, and I only truly understood that when I made the decision to come back.

*

From there, my fight was made up of decision after decision. Only a few days later I got my next big suicidal urge, but as it came on I sat and said to myself, 'Jazz, this decision you are about to make can either continue you towards your dream future, or put you in another cycle of hospital admissions (or worse).' For the first time I sat with these feelings, rather than making an impulsive decision and actioning my urges. I halted my thoughts as they threatened to run away with me. Despite every part of me wanting to run, I made the decision to fight.

Each time this happened, I messaged Wayne and Libby and told them I was struggling. They would respond lovingly and encourage me to do the things I needed to in order to get out of these thought patterns—things like reading over the lists I had written, hanging out with a friend or watching a comedy show.

Over the next few weeks and months, I made more and more decisions that meant reaching out earlier, decisions that taught me how to fight and decisions that ultimately saved my life. These decisions had to be made every single day. Every time my mind would tell me I was a burden and I would impulsively want to run away, every time I would start writing a suicide note or gathering methods, I had to stop and think to myself: 'What are the consequences of this decision I am about to make? Does it get me closer to, or further away from, my future?'

Making fight-fuelled decisions is hard, and a continuous journey. But I can tell you that ever since that decision I made on Christmas Eve to not be a statistic, I have never tried to take my life again.

Your life doesn't change based on the actions of others, but because of your own decisions. Your decisions have the ability to change everything.

Section Four

SAVIOUR

CHAPTER TWENTY-EIGHT

Saviour?

In the previous chapters we talked about decisions, and how my decisions ultimately saved me. In all honesty, this has been a rather new discovery for me—something I've only come to terms with in the last couple of years.

In 2014, when Genevieve Mora and I initially started Voices of Hope and I was telling my story, I used to always say that *Esther* saved me—that the conversation we had that I wrote about right back at the start of this book 'saved my life'. But now I realise that while that conversation certainly sparked the events that led to my freedom from depression and suicidal thoughts, saying and believing that it was *one person* who saved me was more detrimental than I realised at the time. And this belief of thinking that someone could save me almost destroyed me when I stepped into the shoes of trying to save someone else.

In 2014, I wrote about my story for a post on a Facebook page called 'Humans of South Auckland'. In it, I talked about my upbringing, my mental-health struggles and how Gen and I had set up Voices of Hope as a website to help other people. A girl called Jess saw it, and she messaged me to say she felt her story was really similar to mine. She thanked me for sharing my story and for giving her hope.

At this stage I wasn't inundated with messages like I am now, so I saw her message right away. Jess told me that she wanted to share her story, and that she would email it to me. But then I didn't hear from her again.

Instead, a couple of weeks later I got another Facebook message from her, saying she had spent the last week in a coma following another suicide attempt. We kept messaging every now and then, and she would ask me for advice about how to handle her emotions, thoughts and feelings. I remember feeling pretty worried about her, knowing that she was going through so much but feeling like there wasn't a lot I could do to change it.

Then one afternoon at about 2p.m. I got a message saying 'I can't do this anymore.' I called her, and quickly realised that she very much was not OK, so I called the police and told them where she was and that I feared she was currently trying to take her life. I was out of town with some friends, but on our way back to Auckland that night I stopped by the hospital to see her. She lay on a hospital bed, staring at the wall, with her parents sitting on chairs beside the bed. This was the first time I ever met her in person.

That meeting is what really launched Jess and me into the friendship we had. It wasn't a normal kind of friendship, where we would just hang out. Jess was a few years younger than me, and all of our contact involved me helping her when she was struggling. There were many times that I physically pulled her off bridges or out of trees. I became like a mentor to Jess—I understood what she was going through to a degree, and so I did everything I could to try to help her. At times it was hard because I would look at her and remember the feelings and emotions I had going on when I was in her shoes.

After a few months of knowing Jess, one night she messaged me saying that it was time for her to go and that she had planned her disappearance. I wasn't far from where she said she was, so I drove over to try to find her. On the way, I texted her stepmum, Anne, and told her what was going on, and she drove over to join me.

This was the darkest time of my life, but it was also the catalyst for me deciding to make real changes and take control.

I called Jess's cell phone, trying to figure out where she was. She wouldn't answer for a while, and then on about the fifth try she answered my call. By this stage I had made it to the area that she was in, and as it was a quiet night I stood in the street trying to listen for her voice or any clues on her end of the phone as to where she was. Eventually I found her in a little forest area near her house. I pulled her out of the bush and took her to her stepmum's car. As I walked away, Anne said to me, 'Jazz, there are many different people who have tried to help Jess and it has just made things worse. But I think you could be the one that saves her.'

I took this on, thinking that I had to try and save her. To be honest, I think I felt so much pressure to save her because at that stage, in 2014, I believed that Esther had saved me. So if she had saved me, then I needed to be able to do the same thing for other people.

I gave my everything to try to help Jess. At times it actually became more detrimental than good, because I was putting a saviour cape on myself, thinking that I had to be the person to save her—which meant that if Jess ended up in hospital or anything went wrong, then I would feel like I had failed both Jess and her family. But the reality was that I couldn't save her. And I didn't.

*

On 22 April, 2015 at 11a.m. I was sitting in a management meeting for the gym I was working at when I saw a message pop up on my phone. It was another goodbye message from Jess, this time saying 'I'm sorry Jazz for failing you and letting you down. Thank you for everything you have done for me. I love you, I'm sorry, goodbye.'

I had received so many messages like this from Jess before and I knew she had always been OK in the end, so I thought 'I'll just finish the last few minutes of this meeting and then call the police.' So as soon as we finished the meeting I ran down to the office, called the police and messaged Anne. I had tried to message Jess back asking where she was, but she had gone offline by this stage.

I didn't have a car at the time so I couldn't go out and help them look for her. The police suggested that I stay at work and keep near my phone, so I could let them know if I heard anything else from her.

I remember feeling more and more sick as the time Jess was missing grew longer. In the past she had usually been found quite quickly, but this time everything seemed so different. Previously when Jess had sent me goodbye messages, she would still be online when I replied and we would go back and forth for a while until the police found her. This time after she sent the message she went straight offline and nobody could get back in contact with her.

Eventually I left work and went home, keeping in close communication with Jess's parents and friends, who were all banding together to try to figure out where she was. We exchanged messages, trying to see if anyone had any indication of the places she might have gone. As we listed all the locations we knew of, Jess's parents gave them to the police for them to search.

That night was a sleepless one. I felt like I was in an eight-hour panic attack, where my chest was so tight I was struggling to breathe. I had such a heavy feeling of guilt, wondering if we would have found her by now if I had replied right away, or if I had said something different or done something different.

As the sun rose the next morning I was filled with a sinking feeling that this time, Jess wasn't coming home. I was trying so hard to hold onto hope, thinking maybe she had just run to someone's house and she would turn up today. I made myself get up and get ready for work—I didn't really want to go in, but I knew that I needed to try to distract myself somehow.

I gave my everything to try to help Jess. But the reality was that I couldn't save her. And I didn't.

All day we still hadn't heard anything, but then in the afternoon my phone started ringing. It was Anne. When I answered, she said, through tears, 'Jazz, they found her. It's not good.' I immediately knew what she meant. Tears started to stream down my face and I ran out of the office and all the way home.

A million thoughts were running through my mind: why didn't I do this?

Why didn't I do that? I felt so guilty about Jess's passing that when people began to ask me about what had happened I lied and said that I didn't see her message in time. I knew I had seen it, right away, but those few minutes I had waited to call the police were eating away at me. I felt like I was supposed to have been the one who could save her, but instead it was while I was mentoring her that she died.

My mind spiralled out of control. I read back over our messages, looking for everything I had said wrong. Jess had written me a long card thanking me for everything I had done a few weeks before she had passed away and I clung to it, trying to get rid of the guilty feelings. But it wasn't working.

I felt so guilty about her passing, so guilty that I couldn't save her. I spent so long wishing that she had had someone else to help her—thinking that if she had had Esther, Wayne or Libby mentoring her then she would still be here. These feelings really played into my distorted beliefs of being worthless, comparing myself to those who had helped me and feeling like I had really failed Jess.

*

The process of dealing with the guilt of Jess's passing was a long one for me, and to be honest, it is probably something that will always play on my mind. I spent months after she died reading back over our conversations, looking for anything I said or did wrong; feeling like it wasn't fair that she was gone and I was still here and wanting to take her place. I watched her family and friends' hearts break and I felt somewhat responsible for that, because I was supposed to be her mentor, I was supposed to be the person she turned to when she felt like this, and I was supposed to save her.

All the things that I thought I had dealt with came back to the surface, and it wasn't long before I was trying to take my own life again. The next few months it was suicide attempt after suicide attempt after suicide attempt. Remember the story I told you about the police officer Constable Campbell? That happened a few months after Jess passed way. When they found me trying to take my life, I had the card Jess wrote me in my pocket, holding onto it tightly.

It was Jess's passing that led to me leaving church, running away from everyone, trying to move to Australia and my final suicide attempts. My psych ward notes from this time talk about my guilt about losing Jess. It was the darkest time of my life, but it was also the catalyst for me deciding to make real changes and take control.

CHAPTER TWENTY-NINE

Jessica's Tree

While I was in the ward and engaging in therapy, I had the opportunity to work through what had happened with Jess. I always had a deep desire to help people, but I remember one of the nurses in the ward once saying 'Jazz, you can't help anyone until you help yourself.' She was right. Gen and I had originally started Voices of Hope in 2014, wanting to bring hope to people struggling, but I was still dealing with my own demons. If I wanted to work in the area of mental-health advocacy, then I had to deal with my own stuff first—my distorted beliefs, my underlying need to 'save people' because I felt I had to, and how to change my behaviours and responses to my emotions.

With the help of professionals and those around me, I did learn how to fight through all of that, as you read in the first half of this book. The practical journey I took to get from suicidal and being in a psych ward to now speaking hope around the world was a hard one, but once I knew that I was free from my own pain then it was time to really help others.

Following my recovery, Gen and I relaunched Voices of Hope (more on this soon) and I decided to put myself through film school in 2017, to learn how to direct factual content and tell stories that matter. The first story I knew I wanted to tell was Jess's. She had always told me she wanted to tell her story, that she wanted to be a voice of hope—and while at the time she said it she believed she would be here to do it herself, I knew that even though she was gone, her story could still really open up the conversation around mental health and create the change she wanted to see.

At first, I was just going to tell her story for my final film school project, a nine-minute short documentary. I spent every lunchtime working on it from as soon as the course started—I was usually the first to arrive at school and the last to leave.

You are not a superhero. You don't have to save those around you. But what you can do is care, love them and teach them how to fight.

About four months into the course, my tutors asked me if I would be interested in pitching my idea about Jess's story at the annual Doc Edge pitching contest. This is an annual forum where documentary directors from around the country pitch their ideas to a panel of producers, funders and broadcasters. They had never taken someone my age before, let alone a film-school student, but they allowed me to pitch because they thought that story was strong.

I cleared it with Jess's parents and started working on the pitch. As the day got closer, every part of me wanted to drop out. I was so scared of failing and felt so overwhelmed by trying to organise my pitch while also doing everything else in film school (I actually did try and drop out the day before the pitch, but thankfully my tutor wouldn't let me!).

When I arrived on the day I found there were about 25 other people pitching—all of whom had done this before, all of whom had experience and detailed PowerPoints and all of whom were a lot older than me! The judging panel was made up of about 40 people, and all the others who were pitching were also allowed to stay in the room as each person got up. I was second to last to go, and as I got up I was introduced as 'the student who is here to get experience'—basically saying 'She has no idea what she is doing, so be nice.'

I stood there and I told this panel about Jess and about New Zealand's staggering suicide statistics. I told them why I wanted to tell her story, and how my story in a way mirrored Jess's, so I knew how to tell it in a way that would create impact.

The panel was stunned, and at the end of the day I was announced as the winner of the pitch competition. Jess's story was going to be made. It felt pretty surreal, almost like one of those golden-buzzer *X-Factor* moments where I felt for the very first time that maybe this was something I could actually do with my life—that telling stories that create impact was a possible career for me.

After a lot of meetings, I eventually settled on the producers Cass Avery and Alex Reed from Augusto, to help me tell Jess's story, and we got to work. I left film school (as you read earlier, they still let me graduate!) and started working full-time on what would become my web series *Jessica's Tree.*

*

When I pitched the story, I had thought that I was over the guilt already, but as I went through the process I slowly began to realise that I very much wasn't. I put so much pressure on myself to get Jess's story right because I felt like I owed it to her and I was so scared of failing. Don't get me wrong—all of me wanted to tell this story to create change, but the feelings of wishing I had saved her fogged my vision many times through the process.

There was only so much that I could have done for Jess, but I

now know that *it is never our job to save people.* **That is an impossible expectation that we put on ourselves that fuels a vicious cycle of guilt.**

It wasn't until I sat down with every person who I chose to interview for the web series that I realised that everyone felt that way. Everyone felt like they didn't do enough, or that if they hadn't missed something in a conversation or the tone of a text message they could have changed the outcome.

The night after I filmed my interview with Jess's best friend Kylie, I sat at home and reflected on my last few years. Hearing her talk about the guilt she carried made me look back on my own story. What *had* saved me from being another suicide statistic? Was it a person? A conversation? What was it?

As I sat on my bed thinking this over, I realised that it actually wasn't one thing, one person or one conversation that saved me. All of those things were vital to my recovery, but what saved me was *me.*

I could have taken the conversation I had with Esther about surviving and fighting and left the room and not done anything about it. I could have chosen to not walk back into church when I did, or to not open up to people. But through the love and support of those around me (alongside therapy and all those other kinds of things), I was taught how to fight for myself.

There was only so much that I could have done for Jess, only so much that everyone around her could have done—and while we all probably could have done more, I now know that *it is never our job to save people.* That is an impossible expectation that we put on ourselves that fuels a vicious cycle of guilt.

You are not a superhero. You don't have to save those around you. *But what you can do is care, love them and teach them how to fight.* This was a long and hard realisation to come to, but I am so thankful that *Jessica's Tree* turned into something that was not only a tool for society, but also really helped me along the way.

*

In March 2019, *Jessica's Tree* was released into the world via the *NZ Herald* online. I had no idea what to expect, but it quickly become one of the most watched web series ever made in New Zealand. It was on the front page of the paper and being talked about on radio and TV shows, at first here in New Zealand and then it quickly got picked up around the world. It was such an amazing feeling seeing this thing that had been created from such a heartbreaking beginning do so much good in the world.

After *Jessica's Tree* was released, I couldn't tell you how many thousands of messages I got from people saying that it had saved their lives. At first it was overwhelming—I was literally getting people handing me blades and suicide notes in the street! I had parents asking me to go and see their children in hospital, and people reaching out on all forms of social media. I found this hard, especially having taken on the new mental-health model of not trying to be a saviour.

However, one particular message made everything click. It went like this:

Hi Jazz,

I hope you don't mind me emailing you. I just wanted to message you to say thank you.

On Monday I had made the decision to take my life. I've been struggling with depression and PTSD for 3 years (I'm 17) and I had finally given up. I wrote my suicide note and was just waiting for my mum to leave for work so I could go through with it. I sat in my room mindlessly scrolling social media while I waited for her to go and I came across the trailer for Jessica's Tree. I watched it and just bawled my eyes out. Something clicked, and as I watched Jess's friends and family I realised I couldn't do it. I couldn't kill myself.

I ran out to my mum and told her everything and now we are going to get help. Thank you so much for what you do, and thank you for creating Jessica's Tree — it just saved my life.

Kind regards

I sat reading this and I started sobbing. I felt so incredibly proud of this girl and her strength to keep going and keep fighting. I then realised that I hadn't saved her and *Jessica's Tree* hadn't saved her—*she had saved herself. Jessica's Tree* had offered her an opportunity to see hope, but it was *her decision to act on it* that saved her life.

You are stronger than you know. You are stronger than your mind lets you believe.

She could have still chosen to take her life after watching it but *she* chose not to. *She* chose to fight, *she* chose to message, *she* chose to tell someone.

I never saved anyone. I simply created a tool that people could use to help save themselves. This has become a pillar in the work that I do personally and with Voices of Hope. I am not a hero, I am just an everyday, normal person who has lived through experiences that taught me how to fight.

And so, to those who are reading this book who have struggled through suicidal thoughts, thank you for still being here. Thank you for choosing to get up every single day, even though everything inside of you doesn't want to. You are stronger than you know. You are stronger than your mind lets you believe.

I know this because of the simple fact that you are still alive and fighting, and it was your decisions in amongst the chaos that meant you are here today and reading this book. Keep fighting—you've got this.

CHAPTER THIRTY

What's our responsibility?

The previous chapters bring up an interesting question. How do we help people while still equipping them so they can gain the confidence to begin to fight for themselves? It can be hard to figure out the difference between helping someone and stepping into saviour mode.

While I was making *Jessica's Tree* I discovered something that I think is one of the keys for helping our young people. All of Jess's friends talked about secrets—the kind of secrets Jess would make them keep about her hurting herself, her plans to take her life and everything else that was going on for her behind the scenes. Travelling and speaking in schools all around the world, I have come to understand that this is actually a really common thing in every single school.

Friendships are filled with all types of secrets, but these kinds of secrets are the ones that unintentionally put a saviour mask on the person keeping them. The friend often feels the weight of the responsibility of needing to save their friend. They might believe that they are the only one their friend is talking to, and that that they have to keep this secret in order to keep their friend or to not make their friend angry with them. However, as Jessica's friends found out, keeping those secrets didn't help her. In the words of one of her friends who I interviewed for the documentary, 'I would rather have Jess here now and angry at me than not have her here at all.'

There are two things wrong with keeping these kinds of secrets, the first being that saviour mentality. It is so important for you to know that you cannot save someone, as much as we want to believe we can. It takes a community of people to work together to help someone learn how to fight. The second is that it can actually prevent someone from getting the help they need.

When I was struggling, I had a few different people I would talk to. I would usually tell each one a different part of the story, and ask each person to not tell anyone else. This meant that no one really knew how much I was really struggling, and I could keep my protective walls up. I was afraid that if they knew the extent of what was really going on, then they would hate me as much as I hated me.

Things only started to change for me when the people I was talking to began to work together. They pieced together the extent of what was going on, and realised that I was struggling more than I was telling each individual person. Wayne, Libby and Esther already knew each other so they were talking (in a non-gossiping way), and then they also started communicating with the mental-health care team I was under, ensuring that I was being truthful all round and that my care was filled with consistent messaging. For example, if my counsellor thought it was a good idea for me to give my medication to someone to hold and distribute to me daily, I wasn't able to get away with telling Wayne, Libby or Esther that I was safe to keep it on me. Because of this, I was able to get the help I didn't necessarily want, but most definitely needed.

This idea of secret-keeping implies that we alone can and need to save our friends. But that is not our job. Our job is to love people, to speak hope and to be consistent. The second we believe that we as individuals can save someone it becomes dangerous for both you and the person you are trying to help, especially if something goes wrong.

Sometimes we do have to help carry people when they feel they can't fight for themselves, but this should never be a long-term solution.

It is a hard concept to come to terms with, and trying to find the balance between keeping friends' secrets and knowing when you need to seek help from others can be difficult. There are secrets that can be kept in friendships, like what boy you like. But the kinds of things that *cannot* be kept a secret are things like someone self-harming or having suicidal thoughts, or if they are in danger, either from themselves or others.

If I had a dollar for every time that I asked someone not to tell anyone else that I was wanting to kill myself, I would be rich! But others keeping that secret for me, even with the best possible intentions, did nothing for me except keep me in that place.

If you are in school then you need to tell a teacher or a dean, and if you are no longer in school, then always seek advice from someone older and wiser—your parents, a boss, a mentor, a pastor, an aunt or uncle. Even if you think it will make your friend angry with you, it is better that they are alive.

I never suggest that you blindside someone who is struggling with this, though—it can make them feel like you are backstabbing them or gossiping behind their back. I will always tell the person first that I am going to talk to someone else about their struggles, and tell them who it will be. Keeping communication open is key if you don't want them to isolate themselves from you after you talk to someone.

Sometimes we do have to help carry people when they feel they can't fight for themselves, but this should never be a long-term solution. It disables people from learning how to fight and ultimately can block their freedom. It is all about finding the balance.

*

One day in 2014 I was at home sick, and I fell asleep sitting up in bed with my laptop on my stomach. I woke up feeling like I was going to throw up, so I threw my laptop and blankets onto the other side of the bed and ran to the bathroom.

After I was sick I went down to the kitchen to get a glass of water. About 10 minutes later I walked back up to my bedroom. As I approached my door I saw smoke coming out from under it. I didn't quite click as to why that might be happening, so I opened my door.

A huge heatwave hit my face. My laptop had overheated and exploded, and now my whole room was bright orange, filled with flames. I started screaming, alerting my flatmates to the danger, and we all ran out of the house.

That day I lost absolutely everything that I owned. I was only 18 and I didn't have insurance, so when I say I lost everything, I mean *everything.*

That night I stayed at my friend Lisa's house, and after dinner Esther came over. She hugged me as she walked in, then after talking for a few minutes she said, 'OK, Jazz, so you need to go and get your birth certificate and passport and driver's licence replaced.' I remember blurting out something along the lines of 'I can't think about that now!' But Esther said, 'What is wallowing in this hurt going to do? You need to look forward and act on the things you can control.'

What you have to understand is that at this point Esther knew me really well. She knew my tendency to dwell on things and to be over-dramatic and over-emotional. Yes, my house had just burned down, but if Esther hadn't given me the logical alongside the love I probably would have dwelled in the sadness for months.

It is important for you to know that you cannot save someone, as much as we want to believe we can. It takes a community of people to work together to help someone learn how to fight.

This kind of love was echoed throughout our friendship. She would frequently ask me the question, 'So what are you going to do about it?' At the time, I hated it. But as I began to get better I realised how thankful I was for it.

Matching tough love with compassionate love is vital. I am so thankful that Esther was the kind of person who refused to let me live and dwell in my struggles. She also didn't just hand me solutions, but taught me how to find them myself.

A while ago I was sitting in Esther's lounge, talking about those moments, and I began to thank her for teaching me how to fight. She said, 'If someone is drowning, you don't just love them out of it. You teach them how to swim, so that if they ever get into a position like that again they know how to get out of it, and they know how to prevent it from happening.'

This is an incredibly powerful statement. I think that often while we have the best of intentions, we sometimes simply throw out a life raft to those struggling, so they never actually have to learn how to swim. They get so used to being 'saved' by the raft that eventually they forget that it is even *possible* for them to swim. So if you know someone for whom suicidal ideation or self-harm is a long-term habit that doesn't seem to be changing, then it may be time to try a different approach.

Moving from 'rescue mode' to 'collaborative teaching mode' can be hard, because our natural instinct as humans is to jump in and help the people we love, but we must find balance. Using the analogy that Esther used, it is far more beneficial to teach someone how to swim before they get out of their depth, rather than watching them get in trouble then rescuing them every time. That doesn't mean that you won't be there to pull them out if they do start to drown, but it does mean that you are walking alongside them and asking the questions:

- How do we get out of this?
- What are the practical things that you can do right now to fight this?
- What are the things we can do *before* you get to the point of drowning?
- Who else can help you move towards a valued future?

I am so thankful that Esther chose to use tough love when tough love was needed. She loved me enough that she refused to let me go around in circles, but she was also there when I did need help.

Obviously, everyone is different and responds differently to situations, so if you are trying to help someone then you will need to figure out what works best for them. I have found that this particular approach works really well for those struggling with depression, anxiety, suicidal thoughts, self-harm and Borderline Personality Disorder.

Don't ever think that someone is too far gone or that they are too messed up to be saved. I am proof that your consistency, combined with being taught how to fight and make good decisions, can lead to freedom.

Our responsibility is to love, to challenge and to do all that we can to ensure that we teach people how to fight. Compassion is key, but so is action. Love someone enough to refuse to let them continue to live the way they are.

Section Five

FORGIVENES

CHAPTER THIRTY-ONE

Why forgiveness is important

One of the most powerful things I was ever taught was that unforgiveness is a poison that prevents you from growing. I actually first heard this in church, when someone was talking about the impact of unforgiveness towards other people. We can spend so much of our time thinking about the people who hurt us, ruminating over all the bad things they said or did and gripping onto those things, that it can prevent us from being able to reach our full potential.

Once I had started to engage in the battle for my life, I began to realise that I could only get so far without forgiving those who had hurt me. Forgiving didn't mean forgetting what they had done, but it did mean releasing myself from the pain they caused me, and choosing to not let what they had done in the past control my future. Whether it was the sexual abuse, the bullying and harassment or even teachers telling me that I was never going to achieve anything in my life, all of these things bound me for so long, it was almost like I used them as an excuse to stay unwell.

Unforgiveness can cause all kinds of issues. Holding on to unforgiveness can lead you to have bursts of anger, be impulsive, not take responsibility for your feelings or actions and much more. One of the biggest is self-hatred. It can lead to a toxic brew of guilt, shame, self-judgement and self-sabotage. This may seem a bit harsh, because when someone hurts you, you are not at fault—but it *is* up to you how you let it affect you.

Unforgiveness leaves us pointing fingers and continuously blaming others for our pain and actions, instead of taking responsibility for our own lives and emotions. The way people act towards us can trigger a chain reaction of emotions and reactions—for example, if you get into a fight with someone close to you and they say something hurtful, you might have every reason to storm off, but that often doesn't help anything, and just leaves both people feeling bad.

You don't have to tell the other person that you forgive them, or re-engage with them about what happened—it is something that can be done solely from your side.

In all honesty, what I have found in my own life is that the biggest thing about not forgiving people is that it gives us an excuse to not move forward. It ties us to our past, and there is only so far that we can go while holding onto the rope that attaches us to things that have already happened.

For those who have been through trauma this can be one of the hardest things to do, but as someone who has been sexually abused and bullied, I can assure you that forgiveness is oh so worth it. It never excuses what the person did to you, but it releases you from being prevented from moving on because of it.

I understand the resistance people have towards forgiving people who have hurt and wronged them. It can feel like you are letting them get away with hurting you and like they have won. For a long time, I would have read something like the above and been like 'Yeah, fine—but you don't know what happened to *me.* You don't know what they did to *me.*' That statement might be true and valid, but by continuing to live with the resentment and anger I never allowed myself to move forward.

The ability to forgive doesn't make you weak—it fills you with so much strength. It allows you to let go of the hurt and pain that is holding you down. The more that you learn how to forgive those who either intentionally or unintentionally hurt you, the more inner strength you will develop.

The great thing is, you don't have to tell the other person that you forgive them, or re-engage with them about what happened—it is something that can be done solely from your side. Then you can continue to move on with your life without the attachment to the hurt and anger.

*

Forgiving people who hurt you can be a long process, and for some people it may never really end. For most of my life I hadn't been able to forgive those who hurt me. Part of it was me wanting to justify my continued pain—it felt like an explanation to myself about why I felt so bad and why I acted the way that I did. So one day I decided to make a list of the people who had hurt and wronged me, so that I could start the process of forgiveness, setting myself free from having to carry this anger and sadness around with me.
The ability to forgive doesn't make you weak—it fills you with so much strength. It allows you to let go of the hurt and pain that is holding you down.

And there were so many people to forgive! There were kids in school who had bullied me, creating detrimental beliefs; teachers who had told me I was worthless and an attention-seeker; counsellors who had told me I was a lost cause; family members who had hurt me and peers who had taught me that I was a waste of space. Then there were the men who sexually abused me, the people who let it happen, and the people who didn't do anything to punish those responsible. There was my dad, who walked away from me and never came back. The people who told me to go kill myself, and the girl who once gave me a rope to do it (yes, that really happened).

Once I had written out this list I felt quite overwhelmed: I didn't think it was possible to forgive all of these people at once. So instead I began trying to forgive one group at a time.

I started with the kids who had bullied me at school. Considering I went to a total of seven schools, that amounted to a lot of kids, so I sat in my room writing down the names of all of the ones I remembered who had hurt me. Then I began to write a letter of forgiveness to them. I tried to think about what might have made them act that way and show them compassion for their own struggles, even as they had contributed to my own.

To the eight-year-old girl who told me that I wasn't pretty enough to sit with at lunchtime — I am so sorry that you learnt how to put people down at such a young age.

To the boy who stole my shoes and then wrote the word 'ugly' on them in black marker — I am sorry that somewhere in your life you experienced something that taught you how to diminish a young girl.

To the girls who made social media pages about me, who pushed me in the hallways, said hateful things and ensured I hated school — I am sorry that there was so much going on in your life that your anger burst out onto other people. I hope that you have learnt kindness and that you have been able to overcome the issues that made you think it was OK to hurt someone in the ways that you did.

I also forgive you. I forgive you because the reality is that I don't know what was going on in your lives. I don't know about your home lives, your parents or your siblings. But I do know that no one is born a bully.

So instead of holding hatred, I choose to understand and forgive. I am not the words you said to me, and those past events do not define me.

Jazz

I didn't intend to actually send this letter anywhere—it was just something

I wrote for myself to try to get everything down on paper and release my emotions. I didn't even know where to start to get in touch with these people anyway, and I also didn't really want to. My forgiveness of them wasn't for their sake, but for my own.

*

A few months after I wrote this letter in my journal, I received a message from a girl who had been one of my main bullies in primary school. At this stage my story had become public following the initial launch of Voices of Hope and I had a heavy presence in the media, so she had seen me and read about me.

In her message she apologised for bullying me, saying that she had no idea what was going on for me at the time. She said that she had also been in and out of the CYFS system—she had actually been taken out of her home when she was at primary school and placed in a foster home for a while. She told me that she didn't know how to handle her anger, so when she came to school it poured out onto me.

I welled up with tears as I read it. I was beginning to realise that people hadn't been hurting me for who I was, but *because they didn't know how to handle their own emotions or problems.* Kids are told this a lot at school—that bullies cut you down only to make themselves feel taller. But when you are in the middle of it, it never feels like that. It feels like there is something wrong with you and who you are.

Now I knew that this girl and I had been facing similar issues, and we simply responded differently. That didn't make her a bad person, just a broken one ... like me, and so many others. There are times that we will never understand why people bully, and sometimes the people don't even know themselves. In those kinds of situations it is important we remember that our identity is not defined by the words of others, and hold on to the power of forgiveness.

CHAPTER THIRTY-TWO

The hardest to forgive

Understanding why people bullied me and forgiving them was one thing, but forgiving those men who had sexually abused me was a whole other can of worms. This is something I battled with for years. These men had taken not only my innocence as a child, but also warped my identity.

Nothing excuses abuse, ever—but I knew that if I was going to try to move on with my life then I needed to try my hardest to forgive them. Not for them, but for me. While I was holding on so tightly to what had happened, it was impossible for me to look forward, as I was always glancing back at everything they had done wrong.

I don't think I will ever know why these men did what they did. But one night as I was sitting in a church service I had a moment when I thought back on how I had lost the last 19 years of my life because of these men, and I realised I didn't want them to take any more. I once heard someone say 'the best payback you can give the person who hurt you is to live the most incredible and fulfilled life'. So as I sat in this service, I made the decision that I didn't want these men to have any more of my life—it was time for me to forgive them so that I could move on.

While I was holding on so tightly to what had happened, it was impossible for me to look forward, as I was always glancing back at everything they had done wrong.

Forgiving them was a decision made in a moment, but it was a long process. Once again, it came back to my decisions: I had to choose to forgive them again every day. I would often struggle with blurred flashbacks from the abuse, and as these came up I had to literally repeat 'I forgive you' over and over again, out loud.

I hated doing this for a long time—it felt unnatural and like I was letting them win, but it wasn't. It was me learning how to cut the rope that kept me tied to their actions.

I was lucky enough to have Wayne in my corner throughout this entire process, as he was able to teach me what a father figure was supposed to be like. He and Libby, alongside my therapist, really helped me work through what these men had done and begin to understand that I was not defined by the abuse. As I've said, it will never excuse them, but forgiving these men has enabled me to walk with my eyes set on the future, not on the past and these people who took so much of my life with their horrible acts when I was a kid.

I think that the hardest person to forgive, however, has been my biological dad—the man who walked out on me and never once bothered to make contact with me until the day I reached out myself ... and proceeded to block me out of his life again after one conversation. The man who literally created me, yet thought that I wasn't even worth getting to know.

Every little girl wants her dad's approval, and instead I grew up wondering why mine couldn't love me. Why he didn't even like me enough to maybe one day call. Growing up, I never celebrated a single Father's Day. I didn't even know what the man looked like. Forgiving a man that I didn't even know was one of the hardest things I have done to date.

In 2017, I managed to find one of my older half-siblings that I grew up with until I was about six, through social media, and she knew a lot more about him. I began asking her all kinds of questions about him and his past, trying to understand why he didn't want me.

Forgiving others is not usually a one-off thing. Often it requires you forgiving over and over and over again.

She told me that he had had an extremely rough upbringing himself—sexually abused as a child, on drugs at a very young age and dealing not long after that. Hearing these small parts of his story made me begin to understand that he was a very, very broken man. And while his actions will never be excused, I guess for the first time I kind of understood why he was the way that he was. They do say that abuse is a vicious generational cycle, and often those who are the abusers have suffered abuse themselves.

It was interesting to learn more about my biological father, but it wasn't until I met Wayne and Libby that I was really able to begin the process of forgiving him. I think that was because I didn't ever really know what a dad was supposed to be like, and so without understanding what I was missing, I didn't see the extent of the damage he had done.

As I got to know Wayne and he began to step into a father-figure role, I slowly began to see everything that I had missed as a young girl. Wayne taught me that I was never meant to be hurt, that I should never be alone and that I was worth the effort and consistency of a father's love.

Wayne's consistency in showing me what a father was supposed to do led to celebrating my very first Father's Day in 2018. Usually I hated Father's Day—it was always just a reminder of everything that I didn't have, but this time it was different. I spent the whole week leading up to it trying to find a present for Wayne, and not knowing what to get because I had never in my life bought a Father's Day gift! I settled on a lap desk for his laptop, because he always worked late on the couch.

Wayne and Libby's family—their actual family and the 'adopted' ones like myself—got together on the day and celebrated Wayne. I remember sitting on the floor in the lounge watching the room fill with laughter and joy—watching Wayne love his own kids and those who he and Libby had brought into their family—and in that moment I chose to forgive my own dad.

I forgave him because I no longer was missing a father, as I had found one who had helped me to untangle all of the warped beliefs my birth father had caused. Also, I realised that I would never know the extent of my dad's story. I would never know if he ever got to sit in a room like I was at that point, surrounded by family who loved and cared about him. As the saying goes, 'Hurt people hurt people.' My dad was hurt, he was broken and I wasn't going to spend any more of my time allowing the actions of his brokenness cause the pieces of my heart to remain broken.

Choosing to forgive my dad allowed me to go into Father's Day without spite and anger. It was the first year that I didn't get angry or upset, but instead was just so excited to be celebrating Wayne alongside his family and the other 'adopted' kids.

This decision has played a huge part in my healing. In 2019 I again celebrated Father's Day with Wayne and Libby and their family, and I wrote this post on social media:

It's Father's Day in New Zealand today. Father's Day is something I dreaded my entire life. My biological father left when I was three years old and I never saw him again. It was difficult watching others celebrate their dads, feeling like I had missed out. I remember always being the kid who watched as my classmates wrote out Father's Day cards, told their favourite stories and shared the things they loved about their dads.

The last few years I have been so incredibly lucky to have learnt some of the things I missed out on as a kid, celebrating someone who has stepped into a 'father role' in my life. Wayne and his wonderful wife Libby have stepped into parental roles in not only my life, but also the lives of many others, and have walked with me through everything from coming to see me in the ICU of the psych ward, to speaking at our very first Voices of Hope event. They have shown me the kind of love that broke distorted beliefs, and their consistency taught me that I was worth fighting for.

I just spent the last couple of hours strolling through the shops trying to find a Father's Day present and I became so overwhelmed with gratitude that this is something I now get to do (I had never bought a Father's Day gift in my entire life until last year, so I'm still pretty new to it and kinda just walked *around like 'What do you even buy a dad?').*

Father's Day can be a hard day for so many—people who don't have a father, whose fathers have passed or are absent. And so today I am thankful for the men in our world who step up and choose to be fathers—not only to their own children, but to others in their community.

Forgiving others is not usually a one-off thing. Often it requires you forgiving over and over and over again. Forgiving those who hurt me, those who abandoned me and those who abused me was a long and hard journey.

Despite how hard it is, I can say that forgiving those who have wronged you is one of the most powerful things you can do, releasing you from your past and allowing you to be free of it. The men who hurt me warped my identity and the bullies at school made me form false beliefs. By forgiving them I wasn't forgetting what had happened, but I was deciding that their actions didn't rule my thinking anymore. It allowed me to stop looking back at the past, and the hours I spent wishing things never happened turned into hours looking towards the future and everything it could be.

CHAPTER THIRTY-THREE

Forgiving yourself

While forgiving others was a long and hard journey, I think the hardest person to forgive was myself. We tend to be much more critical of ourselves than of other people, and I was always so hard on myself. I hated who I was, who I had become. I despised the three-year-old girl who let men abuse her. I hated the seven-year-old who had let herself get bullied. I hated my every action and response, and looking back at my teenage self, how I had behaved and the things I had done, was one of the hardest things for me, even when I finally became free of mental illness. I was no longer in these vicious cycles of crisis, but I still couldn't forgive myself for the things I did during them.

I remember one day just a year ago when I was working at our church offices. I had become really busy again, overcommitting myself to different roles and jobs, all while still creating content for Voices of Hope. Staying busy was something I used to do when I was stressed out or feeling low, because it meant that I didn't have time to stop and think about all of the bad things. Wayne noticed that I was really busy and was getting stressed by it all, so he pulled me aside and asked if I had gone back into those old habits.

I am not my mistakes. I am not my past. I am fighting for my future—one that is worth fighting for. And I am worth fighting for.

Everything inside of me shut down. I hated the way I used to respond so much, and the thought that Wayne perceived that I was acting like that again crushed me. When he said that, of course he didn't mean that I *had* gone back into all those old habits—he was only acting our of concern and making sure that I was OK—but that isn't the way that my mind had taken it. I felt like I would always be this broken teenage girl in everyone's eyes.

In fact, Wayne was right: I was really busy and had overcommitted myself. He hadn't thought I was back to who I used to be, but was just worried that busyness was an old coping mechanism that I was falling back on.

Wayne saw how much his words had affected me. My face dropped and my eyes filled up with tears. He messaged me later to apologise, and we got together to chat in the auditorium. I burst into tears, telling him how much I hated my teenage self and that even though now I was living a very different life, I still couldn't get past my reactions and responses as a teen.

Wayne turned to me and said, 'Jazz, imagine there is a little sparrow that has been born in a nest in a tree. That little sparrow gets kicked out of the nest before it learns how to fly, and falls into a pile of mud. The sparrow is trying so hard to get out, but is covered in mud. Would you be mad at the sparrow? Would you say "You stupid sparrow, get yourself out?" No, you wouldn't.

I forgave myself. I forgave myself for the crisis behaviour, for lying to people, for always being in hospital, for hurting myself and for

struggling to keep stable friendships.

'You were that sparrow once, Jazz. It wasn't your fault—you didn't put yourself in the mud, but now you have got yourself out and you are only just learning how to fly again.'

I burst into tears, and he pulled me in and hugged me. I had never thought about it like that before. The story of the sparrow really hit on something inside of me: how could anyone be angry at a little baby bird who was hurt and was struggling to get out of the mud it had been thrown into?

I began to use this story as a tool to start the process of forgiving myself. Every time that I started to get annoyed at myself, or I would find myself judging 'old Jazz', I would literally say out loud, 'She was just a baby sparrow.'

*

In 2017, while I was making *Jessica's Tree,* Alex Reed and Cass Avery from Augusto and Bloom Pictures talked to me about making a second documentary, about the process of making *Jessica's Tree*—this time telling my side of the story. It took me a while to agree to it, as it is pretty terrifying having your life put on camera, but I thought that if it might help even one person then it would be worth it.

For two years, I had a camera crew follow me around on my journey of telling Jess's story, capturing every high and every low. They asked me to do video diaries every day, talking about my experiences, unfiltered. This meant I had to battle quite a few things mentally while on camera.

As part of this story, the producers and I wanted to dive back into the details of my own story, looking at how it related to Jess and why I do the work that I do with Voices of Hope. At this stage I was advocating in the media and online, and an overview of my story was being shared all over the world. I was working alongside government agencies to try to create change in the mental-health system, and was speaking in schools and at conferences and events. However, even though I was a strong advocate in the public eye, I was still on my own journey and there were still things I hadn't fully dealt with.

Only a few weeks after I had had the baby sparrow moment with Wayne, the producers asked me to go back through all of my CYFS files and hospital files, as part of telling my own story in the feature film. I hadn't looked at my CYFS files since 2014, when I had gone through them with Nic (see chapter 3), and I had never looked at my hospital files, which I had gained access to only about a month earlier.

It had been a pretty long application process to get my hospital files, which I later discovered was because there was about 2000 pages from Auckland Hospital alone from my teenage years! When they arrived in the mail I didn't really know what to do with them. It felt like the size of two giant phone books, with CONFIDENTIAL plastered over the front of the envelope.

I had taken them up to my room and just stared at the pile for a while before deciding it probably wasn't wise for me to start trying to go through them by myself. So, when the time came that I had to go through them for the film, I decided to read them beforehand at Wayne and Libby's house, so that I had support around me if they became tough to read. The others in the family watched a Harry Potter movie as I sat on the floor of the lounge going through my files.

I read of this girl who was so broken that she was cutting herself in the ward. Who was ending up in hospital almost every couple of weeks with self-inflicted injuries or following suicide attempts.

The files were filled with discharge summaries and extensive doctor and psych assessment notes, and included the notes handwritten by the nurses from the psych ward. Reading the things some of them said about me was heartbreaking. During one of my hospital stays I had tried to take my life in the ward. A nurse found me and responded very badly. I had tried to tell the other nurses what had happened, but because I was in a psych ward, they didn't believe me. Notes following the incident said things like 'During checks, Jazz was found in her room highly distressed. She tried to tell me about X ... I did not engage with this conversation and left the room, putting her on frequent checks.'

That incident did happen, and unfortunately things like that happen more often than the system would like to admit. Knowing other nurses shut down conversation with me and spoke like they didn't believe me was pretty hard. In saying that, there were also many notes where the nurses were so caring, loving and there for me.

As I continued to read through the notes and read more about my behaviour, I felt anger growing inside me—anger and hatred towards the young girl I was reading about. On the night I had been tackled by police off the edge of a cliff and nearly took them down with me, the notes say we all walked into the hospital covered in mud from the fight and I was handcuffed. I read about a time where I had cut myself all over while in my room in the ward, and the nurse had to clean everything up. I read of a girl who would scream at the staff, run away and refuse to eat as a form of control, and who would often have to be restrained by staff.

As I read these accounts from the hospital staff, I began to wonder how on earth this girl had ended up where she was now, and why anyone would ever love her. These files were incredibly hard for me to read, and I didn't know if it was a good idea that I had read them. I could only read them because I was in a space where healing was already underway, I had strategies to manage distressing situations, and good people around me for support. But it also made me feel incredibly humbled to be reminded of where I once was, and so thankful to really know what I had managed to fight through. Sitting there in Wayne and Libby's lounge, it felt like I was reading about another person altogether.

After finally finishing the hospital files, I opened my CYFS files. Re-reading them, I found that I had forgotten a lot of what was in there—partly because I had blocked a lot of it out, but also because I hadn't opened the files again since 2014. Re-reading the statements and interviews with me as a kid and seeing my responses to small things become so dramatic out of fear started to put everything into perspective.

How could anyone be angry at a little baby bird who was hurt and was struggling to get out of the mud it had been thrown into?

As I was reading these files I became overwhelmed with emotion. Wayne, who had been sitting on the couch behind me, came and sat next to me on the ground and wrapped his arms around me. We kept reading together, looking at the stories, the interviews and how these men had hurt me.

For the first time in my life, I saw my teenage self through the eyes of my three-year-old self. I felt compassion for her, I understood her. I had spent my entire teenage years hating myself and the way I acted. I never understood *why* I was like that and would spend night after night wishing that I was someone else. As I read the two sets of files side by side, I could see why I was such a broken teenager.

For the first time in my life, as I was sitting on that lounge-room floor, surrounded by people who cared, I forgave myself. I forgave myself for the crisis behaviour, for lying to people, for always being in hospital, for hurting myself and for struggling to keep stable friendships. Not only this, but I also managed to forgive my three-year-old self.

For some, this may be confusing—why would I need to forgive myself for something that was done to me? But I had always been so angry that I had let that happen to me, and that I had covered up for the men abusing me. I resented that girl because that was the time that changed everything for me. But I now realise that this was all out of my control. I was only a toddler, trying to navigate this big wide world while being taught at that tender age what fear was.

This night is what began the process of forgiving myself. Understanding that I really was just a broken little girl who didn't know any better really put things into perspective for me. On that night, as I sat surrounded by both these files and also Wayne, Libby and their daughter Grace, I knew that I would be OK. I looked around the room and I felt so much love. These people had known me through the times described in the hospital files and they had forgiven my behaviour. I thought that if they could forgive me, and not see me through the filter of my past, then maybe I could, too.

The next day we got out these files again and went through them on camera for the film. I felt prepared for what was to come, and was able to read through them with almost a sense of victory, because while these files were about me, I was now reading them from a place where I got to use all of those bad experiences for good.

Forgiving yourself can be one of the hardest things to do—I know, I didn't manage to do it until 2018! But I have discovered that being able to get to a place of forgiving yourself can release you from so much pain.

I now know that I am not my mistakes. I am not my past. I am fighting for my future—one that is worth fighting for. And I am worth fighting for.

Section Six

DREAM

CHAPTER THIRTY-FOUR

The importance of dreaming

Learning to dream again can be one of the hardest things for people who have been suicidal. When you have lived so long believing that you wouldn't see your next birthday, or turn 20, or have any kind of future life, dreaming can be confusing and difficult. But it is one of the most important things that we can do and that we can teach others to do. It is impossible to fight if you don't know what you are fighting for.

For a long time I couldn't dream. I refused to look at the future because I didn't think I had one. There were times when I would wonder what I might do with my life one day, but for me dreaming was a scary thing, because it meant I risked being disappointed. I would have rather expected nothing than have hoped for something, because that way I stayed in control of not being disappointed or failing.

For years there was one thing on my mind, and that was dying. This didn't mean that at times I didn't have hopes or aspirations—I definitely did. I always wanted to be a kids' TV presenter, because I remember watching kids' TV shows growing up and they were a wonderful escape for me. I would watch these shows and feel such joy, and so as I got older I remember wanting to do the same for others. However, while I would want that deep down, I always lived with the expectation that it would never happen—it was a nice thought, but could never be a reality because I was sure I wouldn't be around long enough to do it.

Dreaming is one of the most important things that we can do and that we can teach others to do. It is impossible to fight if you don't know what you are fighting for.

During the later part of my mental-health battle, dreaming became near impossible. Sitting in the psych ward, surrounded by slightly off-white walls, being dished out medication three times a day and having staff check on me every ten minutes, I found it pretty hard to dream or see any kind of future. But it was while I was in that ward that those closest to me began to speak about my future and began dreaming for me. They began to talk about things that I could do with my life one day, asking questions like 'If you could do anything with your life, what would it be?'

When I was in my final psych-ward admission, I got transferred to the Intensive Care section. You know things are bad when you get moved to the high-care unit of a psych ward! I kept trying to destroy myself physically and run away. I was on so much medication to try to even me out and calm me down, but I was still constantly managing to find ways to hurt myself in my room.

Your future is in the hands of your decisions. Anything is possible if you decide to dream.

In the midst of one attempt, I was found by some nurses. Crying and screaming at the top of my lungs, I shouted to the nurses to just let me die, and resisted them as they tried to grab onto me to calm me down.

I burst out of my room, ran down the hallway that connected the two wards and fell to the ground behind a pillar. I think I was trying to hide, but in hindsight I realise that of course the ward was very small and there really was nowhere to run. The nurses left me there for a while, because there was no possible way for me to get out. I began to calm down a little bit, and eventually a team of nurses came down and asked me if they needed to carry me back to my room or if I would go willingly. I decided in that moment, as much as I didn't want to, to get up and walk with them. I realised I had already caused quite a scene, and now I was a bit calmer I didn't want to carry on with that.

The day following that incident I don't remember at all, because of the strong medication I was given to calm me down. I saw a psychologist that day, and her notes in my hospital records show that she wrote about me being cold and emotionless. However, when I saw her again a few days later I didn't remember meeting her that first time at all. A couple of days later I wrote this in my diary.

It is hard to put into words what goes through someone's mind. If only there was a way to show the images in my head, the thoughts that go in and around my brain. If only there was a way to truly express how much help I need. How broken I am. How no circumstance can help change my mindset because even the most rewarding situations do not fulfil the gap in my mind that says die.

When I was younger, the idea of suicide was something that brought attention to me, and while it wasn't positive attention, it was something. However now, at the age of 20, the idea of suicide has become so real. So real to the point where I have spent the last 27 days in hospital in the mental-health ward fighting for my life. I am trying more than anyone would ever know, trying to discover who I am, trying to 'fix' myself and trying to act like everything's OK when it isn't.

I have made such an incredible mess of my life that every day I wish that I was someone different. Someone normal. Someone who really could do amazing things . . . but instead, all I see is a circle that I go in, a circle that lands me in suicidal thinking at least every few months despite everything seeming OK.

I would give anything to be seen as 'normal'. To be seen as someone who doesn't have these mental issues. I don't even recall a moment in my life where I became like this and I hate that.

I am trying. I really am. My mind is a living nightmare and I feel like I can't escape it. I need help, I really need help, and even though I am currently sitting in a hospital bed, I still do not feel like I am getting the help that I need.

Why am I like this? What happened to me that made me feel like this? That made me react like this, or act in a certain way that pushes others away? Why do I feel like no one could ever love me? I cannot pinpoint where it went wrong ... I wish I could, I wish I could pin it on something but I can't, and that only makes me realise that this is just who I am. That I made me like this ...

Why did I do this? Why can't I stop it? Help me ... Please ... I am drowning in my own mind and I can't stop it.

I was lower than I had ever been before. Life was dark. However, the day after I wrote this was the day I have told you about earlier, when Wayne and Libby came to visit me in the ward. As well as telling me they loved me, they also said something else that really helped to shift my mindset.

Wayne said, 'Jazz, I think that one day your story is going to change the world ... and it is going to be sooner than you think.' I stared at him, then looked around the dirty white-walled room. I was in the ICU of a psych ward—I was at my lowest, it really couldn't get any worse. How could my story ever do anything? But Wayne kept saying it, with both him and Libby telling me they believed in me and that they truly believed that one day my story could create change in the world. That I could *be* change.

What they chose to do that day was believe in a girl who couldn't believe in herself. I left that interview room and went back to my room with those words on replay in my mind. They didn't make sense to me—I was in a worse state than I had ever been in before, but somehow Wayne and Libby chose to believe in me and believe that I had some kind of future.

A few days passed and Wayne's words stayed on repeat in my mind: 'One day your story is going to change the world.' As I began to think on it more and more, a tiny little light sparked inside me, as I realised that maybe everything I had been through hadn't been for nothing. Maybe one day, if I could fight through this, then I could be a part of something greater. I could be part of changing the world. I had no idea at this stage what that would look like, but it gave me a glimmer of hope and something to start dreaming about.

Write down one thing you want to do or see the next day, and then slowly start to work your way up.

I knew that if I was ever going to help other people then I needed to help myself first, and as you have been reading, that was a long process. It was the belief of those around me, of Wayne, Libby and Esther, who chose to see a future that at that stage I couldn't see at all, that enabled me to start to see glimpses of it too. Maybe one day my story *could* change the world.

I decided to not wait until I was mentally well before I started dreaming again. I needed something to work towards, so as I sat in the psych ward I began to write down my dreams. Things that I could do one day when I became well. I wrote down things like travelling the world, and relaunching Voices of Hope. I wrote down things like speaking in schools and at events. I also wrote down dreams of one day having a family of my own and having a good group of friends.

*

This is why dreaming is so important, even if it is just about the next day, or the next week. Dreaming of that beach trip, that sunset, that plane ride or that career. You don't have to jump straight into dreaming everything about your future, but finding something every single day to fight for will do more than you will ever imagine.

When you are in the depths of struggling, it can be so incredibly hard to look to the future, so I encourage you to even just start with the next day. Write down one thing you want to do or see the next day, and then slowly start to work your way up. You need to have something to fight for, whether it's just the next catch-up with a friend or seeing a family member. Something ... anything! It doesn't have to be going out and changing the world, but simply having hope for change. Hope for a moment when you won't feel the way you currently do, because that hope is real.

When it came to dreaming in my own story, it did start with other people dreaming for me—other people choosing to say, 'Hey, Jazz, imagine the next beach trip we can take when you get out of the ward?' or 'Hey, Jazz, what if one day you could go to film school?' If you know someone who is currently struggling, choose to speak hope and a future into them. It may not seem like it is having an impact, but your words and your belief that they can get through this will do more than you will ever know. It isn't an immediate fix, but it is something that can slowly but surely begin to chip away at the thoughts that say, 'What is the point?'

Your future is in the hands of your decisions. Anything is possible if you decide to dream.

CHAPTER THIRTY-FIVE

What stops us dreaming

It is one thing to be told to dream, but it is a whole other thing to then actually start doing it. I think that is because when you live with trauma or mental illness, dreaming seems pointless, and like another opportunity to be let down. We would rather assume our lives will be nothing than dream we could do something, only to then fail.

I think that there are many things in life that stop you from dreaming, or limit your ability to dream. It could be a teacher who tells you that you would never amount to anything, a parent who told you that you were worthless. It might be a failed job, a bad experience or just a fear of failure.

For me, it was a mixture of many things, but I think the main thing that stopped me from having dreams and plans for my future was that I truly believed that my illness was my identity. I believed that this was who I was and who I would always be, therefore it was impossible for me to change or imagine that my life could ever be any different. I lived my life believing that I would die by suicide before the age of 20, so I would never dream about or plan into the future. I didn't think that I had one.

Trying to fight through mental illness without any idea of what it is that you are fighting for, what goal or dream you are trying to reach, will make the journey and battle a heck of a lot harder.

The importance of dreaming is something we should never underestimate, though, because it is still so beneficial to have plans and goals even if you don't reach them right away. Imagine being a solider and going to war but having no idea why or what it is that you are fighting for. I don't think anyone would agree to go to battle under those circumstances. So for you to try to fight through mental illness without any idea of what it is that you are fighting for, what goal or dream you are trying to reach, will make the journey and battle a heck of a lot harder. That is why I talked about the importance of even dreaming just for the next day or the next week—it gives you a target, something that you are working towards.

*

One thing I have discovered through my journey of learning to dream is that what seems like a 'failed' dream doesn't mean it will never happen. As you now know, Voices of Hope originally started in 2014—but it didn't turn out the way I planned that time. Let me tell you the story.

My co-founder Genevieve (Gen) Mora and I first got to know each other in 2013. We were both 18 at the time and had actually never met in person. You see, there was a girl from America who had done a high-school exchange to my school in Timaru. This girl had been to an acting camp with Gen in America, so when she found out that I had a bit of interest in acting and the media industry too, she was like, 'Oh, you have to meet my friend Gen! I think you will really get along well. She's a New Zealander, too!' Gen and I became friends on Facebook but we didn't really talk to each other, just saw posts come up on each other's news feeds. I didn't know anything about Gen's mental-health journey at this time, and Gen didn't know mine—we thought that all we had in common was an interest in the media industry. Little did we know what was about to unfold!

In 2013, a good friend of mine took her life. A few days later I decided to write a social-media post about it. I can't remember exactly what I said, but it was about how heart-wrenching suicide is. Gen saw this come up on her news feed and decided to send me a message. She said how sorry she was that I had lost a friend, and mentioned that she had also battled with mental-health issues. She suggested that we should try to do something to help people like my friend who had just taken her life. To give you some context around this, at this stage there wasn't really anyone talking about mental health openly in media or even in public in New Zealand. There were a couple of people speaking out or sharing their stories here and there, but it was still extremely stigmatised and a topic no one wanted to talk about.

Gen and I got talking about this idea—we knew we wanted to do something around mental health but had no idea what. For the next few weeks we went back and forth on Facebook Messenger—Gen was still living in Los Angeles at the time and I was in Auckland. We had both been very brief with each other that we had our own mental-health battles but didn't dive into it too much—we just knew that we wanted to make change, and spent a lot of time trying to figure out what would have been helpful for us when we had been struggling.

It is OK to fail—but it is so important that you choose to get back up again. Sometimes things won't go to plan and things will seem to fall apart, but don't ever let that stop you dreaming.

We both had a passion for storytelling and media, so we came up with the idea of trying to mash the two together, combining our love of media with a message of hope. At the start we were just thinking of making a blog, filled with inspirational quotes and stories, but over the following weeks it developed into deciding to tell people's stories of surviving mental-health battles through video content.

We were trying to figure out what to call this new idea when one day out of the blue Gen messaged and said, 'What about Voices of Hope?' and I was sold. I loved it. That was exactly what we wanted to be—a voice of hope.

We started to contact people we knew who had had mental-health battles, to gather stories to film. Gen was moving back to New Zealand at the start of 2014, so we thought if we could get planned remotely, then as soon as she got back we could start shooting and launch the site.

Gen flew home to New Zealand, and as two very excited 18-year-olds we decided that we would meet the day that she got back. She hadn't even unpacked her bags but we decided to meet at the Sky Tower in Auckland city to spend the day dreaming and planning.

It was pretty surreal actually meeting her for the first time as we stood underneath the tower. She was way taller than I expected, but we immediately felt like old friends who had known each other for ages. We shared passion, drive and determination and I think that made us bond pretty quickly.

For the next few hours we sat up the top of the Sky Tower, overlooking the city and dreaming of everything we could do. We started locking in shoot dates and set a target of launching one month from that meeting.

In the next few days we set up Instagram and Facebook accounts and started to promote our idea online, using only the hashtag #VOH as a way to get people curious about it. At that stage we were only sharing it with our own friends on social media, so it had a very small following! We spent time googling ideas and designing a website, and bought two white T-shirts that we ironed Voices of Hope logos onto. We filmed some stories and an intro video, then it finally came time to launch it into the world. We were so excited. We thought we had created something amazing and we were already certain we wanted to do this forever.

I still remember our very first newspaper article in the local paper. It had a photo of Gen and me sitting in a park with huge smiles on our faces and the headline 'Website already creating change'. It was all about what we were doing and why we had decided to create Voices of Hope. It felt incredible to pick up the paper and see this story and our photo in it! People were starting to hear about our message, and that meant people were seeing that hope was real.

The site and campaign got a lot of attention, and a lot of New Zealanders were coming on board and supporting the cause. Both Gen and I were still doing other things full-time (I was at Equippers College and Gen was working at a school), but we were determined to make it work, and spent most weekends filming content.

But as our profile grew (at the time it felt significant, but I realise now it really wasn't—haha!), the pressure grew too, and so did my realisation that I wasn't as well as I thought I was. Both Gen and I were asking people to share their stories, but we still weren't comfortable sharing our own—I still didn't know exactly what Gen went through and she didn't really know what I had been through.

It was during this time that Jess, the girl who I would later make *Jessica's Tree* for, started to message me. Now I was a 'role model' for mental health, I felt huge pressure to try to save her, as I have told you earlier. Her death felt like a huge failure to me.

People were starting to hear about our message, and that meant people were seeing that hope was real.

After Jess passed away and my own mental health began to spiral downwards, I started to drop back on working on Voices of Hope. Gen and I kind of drifted apart, and something that we once worked on every weekend started to slow down. We didn't really talk that much about what was going on, or why we felt this way—we honestly just kind of drifted along, and then one day I messaged her saying 'I think we should take VOH down for a while'. She agreed—she had moved back over to America anyway and was doing other things.

So we announced that we were taking a break on social media. We had no idea if we would ever come back, and to be honest, I felt like a total failure. We thought that we had this amazing thing going and we had failed. We couldn't keep it going—the work became too much and neither of us was ready for it.

It was heart-wrenching. I had felt like I was on the right track, I had found something I wanted to do with my life, yet I wasn't even well enough to keep it going.

*

As you have read, during the next year my mental health spiralled uncontrollably downwards and I tried to take my life more times than ever before. I was so broken and I felt like a total failure. I had no sense of direction or future. I became so afraid of dreaming again, because what if it didn't work out?

What I have learnt through this is that it is OK to fail—but it is so important that you choose to take it as a learning experience *and get back up again.* Sometimes things won't go to plan and things will seem to fall apart, but don't ever let that stop you dreaming.

You've read earlier in this book about the steps that led to my recovery. If I had let the fear of past failure stop me, or let my mind tell me that there was nothing to live for, what happened next would have never taken place—the year that changed everything.

CHAPTER THIRTY-SIX

'Dear Suicidal Me' 2

'Are you guys still thinking of doing Voices of Hope?'

A Facebook message Gen and I received at the end of 2016 sparked something in both of us. We hadn't really talked about relaunching Voices of Hope—partly out of fear, but also out of not knowing what we wanted to do with our lives. It was something that still played in the back of my mind though, especially as I was feeling a lot better and I had worked through a lot of my struggles by this point. I had been in touch with Gen on and off since we took the original Voices of Hope web presence down, and we both knew that we still wanted to help people and to use our stories for good. But we had never really discussed coming back to Voices of Hope until this message came through.

By this stage Gen had moved back to Auckland, and I had come out of my dark spiral and learnt how to fight, combatting my demons once and for all. I was working as a receptionist at a business but was planning on enrolling in film school the following year.

Gen and I began talking on Facebook Messenger, debating whether we should start it up again. We knew that if we chose to do it, we would have to commit this time. We took a few days to think about it and then agreed that this *was* something we wanted to do. The time felt right, both for us and for the wider public in New Zealand—finally people were starting to talk more about mental health.

The time felt right, both for us and for the wider public in New Zealand—finally people were starting to talk more about mental health.

We spent the next few months planning the new Voices of Hope—filming content, collecting stories and redefining what it would be. It was hard at the start to find people to come on board and tell their stories, because most people didn't remember us or the site, and it is a big thing to ask people to go public about their mental-health battles, but we managed to rally together a few of our friends to participate. The message was the same as the first time we launched Voices of Hope: concentrating on the 'hope' and the 'how' of people getting through their battles.

We were determined to ensure we didn't just target one kind of person or illness, so we explored and told stories from as many different people as possible. My story was about my battle with suicidal thoughts, and Gen's was with an eating disorder. It was during the planning stages of this new launch that we decided to actually tell each other our own stories, because we knew that if we were going to ask others to tell theirs then we had to be ready to tell our own.

This is when I found out that Gen's battle with mental illness started when she was just nine years old, when she developed anxiety and obsessive-compulsive disorder (OCD), which began to rule her life. She was so afraid that if she didn't do things an even number of times (like opening a door four times) then someone was going to hurt her. This developed into trying to control anything she could in her life, including food. She began to restrict what she ate, and not long after that she developed anorexia. Eventually she was admitted into hospital so unwell that she was close to death. She fought her battle for a few years, going in and out of the children's psychiatric ward, literally fighting for her life. But she eventually came out on top and beat her anxiety and anorexia.

I realised how incredibly thankful I was to still be standing here, to still be alive and fighting, and now in a place where I could use my story to help other people.

Obviously I had never experienced having an eating disorder so I didn't understand exactly what she had gone through, but I remember being so moved by her story and so heartbroken to find out that *so many people* struggle with this. Knowing how different our own stories were was why we wanted to not just focus on one disorder or condition, but mental health as a whole.

Once we had set our mission and values, we designed our website and began shooting video interviews. It was at this time that I decided to enrol at the South Seas Film & Television School, so I could learn how to direct our content and videos in a way that was powerful and impactful. The one-year course would give me intensive training in film and TV directing. Voices of Hope was still an unpaid gig, so I became a full-time student living on student allowance and Gen went on working at the school, with us both working on Voices of Hope on the side.

About four weeks into the course, I decided to direct my first proper video for Voices of Hope. We knew we needed a good video to launch with and I came up with the idea for what would become *Dear Suicidal Me.* I remember sitting in my tutors' office asking for their advice and their thoughts on my idea. They loved it, so I went ahead with planning and shooting it.

Remember that letter I had written myself in the psych ward—the letter to my future suicidal self? That letter is what inspired this video, but this time the letters were very, very different. For the video, I had four people who had tried to take their lives read out their original suicide notes. I knew two of these people, one was a connection through a friend of a friend, and I was the fourth! The friend of a friend was a guy called Rob Mokoraka. He is an incredible man who made a very public suicide attempt, by walking into the firing range of a police officer while in crisis. I knew his story from the media, and so to have him on this shoot was really incredible. At this stage I had only just learnt how to do all the technical stuff like call sheets and AV scripts (the details of who, what and when for each day, and the scripts that detail what you need to shoot), so I taught Gen how to do this stuff and she stepped into the role of 'producer' while I pulled together the script using everyone's suicide letters.

I then got each one of these people to write a letter entitled 'Dear Suicidal Me'—that was written to their *past* suicidal selves. In these letters they told themselves about all the good things that were about to happen for them, and all of the reasons why they were so glad that they were still alive.

I decided to do this because I wanted people who were struggling to watch it and to relate to it—to relate to the words spoken on the screen and to the letters being read. I knew that as someone who was once suicidal, if I saw something like this then it may have given me hope that it was possible to come out the other side. I often heard people's amazing stories, but I knew from my own experience that even as they talk it can still be so hard to relate to them because you can only see what is right in front of you and not the person who was once struggling. **The message concentrated on the 'hope' and the 'how' of people getting through their battles.**

That is why I decided to get them to read their suicide notes, too. It was a bold move and something that hadn't been done before, but I felt like it was going to be a strong way of engaging those struggling and showing them there is hope. By hearing how these people once felt, and how they felt now, I could show hope in action.

It was pretty hard for me to go back to my own suicide note, the last such note I ever wrote. It made me remember what it was like to be back in that place, but as I read it, it also reminded me that *right now* there were people writing notes exactly like mine and I knew that it was so important for them to not feel like they were alone.

As I sat down to write my future letter, my 'Dear Suicidal Me' letter, I got about two lines in before I started bawling my eyes out. I suddenly realised how incredibly thankful I was to still be standing here, to still be alive and fighting, and now in a place where I could use my story to help other people.

When we released this video on Facebook as part of the launch of the new Voices of Hope, we could have never imagined what happened next. It went viral, and was shared by media outlets around the world. First it hit 100,000 views, and then 1 million, and then 10 million, and now sits at *over 80 million* views worldwide. That single video, inspired by the girl in the psych ward, launched everything we now do for Voices of Hope.

CHAPTER THIRTY-SEVEN

Dream turned reality

The messages we received once we launched the site started to mount up to the hundreds and then the thousands. Very quickly they became my 'why'—the reason I would get up everyday and juggle studying full-time with working on Voices of Hope. The reason I would (and still do) work for Voices of Hope for free. The reason I would give up my nights, weekends and holidays to plan and create content for Voices of Hope. Here is an example of my 'why':

Hi there

My name is Amy and I am a mother from Canada. It has taken me a few weeks to gather myself to send this email as I haven't found the words to express to you.

On March 1st, my 15-year-old daughter walked into my room crying, suicide note in hand, and told me that she needed help. As I held her she told me there was a [suicide method] ready for her, and sure enough, there was. Through her tears she told me that after she [set up the method] and wrote the letter she went on Facebook to message her best friend goodbye.

As she logged into her laptop, at the very top of her news feed was a video one of her friends had shared. That video was your video. She clicked on it, watched it and suddenly realised that she couldn't take her life and that she needed to fight. So instead of [starting the attempt] she came to my room and told me everything . . . about the bullying, how depressed she was but that following the video she felt like there was hope for her.

Now, my daughter is still alive and in therapy because of you. So thank you, for saving her life and for giving her hope.

Keep doing what you do, you are incredible.

It wasn't long before we were on our first high school tour across Australia and New Zealand, sharing our stories of hope and teaching kids how to be resilient. We kept creating videos for Voices of Hope and people started contacting us to share their stories, asking to be a Voice of Hope themselves. Our profile was growing and our message was spreading.

As I have written about in chapter 29, half way through the year that I was studying directing, my tutors put me forward to pitch at the annual Doc Edge pitching forum. As a student, and about 10 years younger than everyone else there, I walked into a room filled with experienced film producers and directors and managed to win the whole thing.

After I was announced as the winner I had every person on the panel coming up to me in the foyer, handing me their business cards and saying they would love to meet with me and work with me on this project. I remember feeling so overwhelmed I didn't even know what to say or how to respond. I eventually got into my car and just started crying.

This isn't a New Zealand issue, but a global one ... and if we want to make real change, we have to begin to work together with other countries and really band together.

I called my tutors from South Seas—who also cried!—and the next day I sat in their office going through the business cards, trying to figure out who I should meet with. It was during this time that I met producer Cass Avery. I met with her for coffee along with another woman, Alex Reed, and something about them just felt right. They seemed so passionate about this subject and this story and they wanted to help me tell it. I decided to go with them, and Cass began to work with South Seas to get me to finish early so that I could start working on this project as soon as possible.

The school was amazing—they let me finish early (while still letting me graduate) and helped me every step of the way while I navigated this new industry. In the first few weeks of working with Cass at her production company, Augusto, an idea was thrown around that this series idea also had potential to be a film. We just didn't know what the film was. Cass suggested that we meet with award-winning filmmaker Leanne Pooley and see what she thought.

We sat down in a back office at Augusto, explaining the idea to Leanne, and within about five minutes she said, 'Oh, I think the series is exactly what Jazz pitched. But the film, I think is about you, Jazz. The film is your story.'

I was stopped in my tracks—Leanne wanted to make a feature film about *me?* My immediate reaction was no way, but as I began to think on it over the next couple of days I realised that if it could help just one person then it would be worth it, so I agreed.

As I have written about earlier in the book, I spent the next two years directing what would become *Jessica's Tree,* all while being followed with a film crew making the feature that would be called *The Girl on the Bridge.* It was pretty overwhelming. Not only was I directing my first-ever series, but I was doing it all under the microscope of a film being directed by one of our most well known and experienced documentary directors.

While all this was going on, I was still working on Voices of Hope, shooting campaigns and starting to be invited to speak at conferences, events and schools in New Zealand and overseas. I also became one of the 'go to' people for media when it came to mental-health stories. My entire life for that two years was all about this subject of mental health, which at times was pretty hard, but so worth it.

One day when I was sitting in the office at Augusto I got a call from a woman I didn't know, who wanted me and Gen to speak at something around mental health. Once we talked about it some more, I found out that she actually wanted Gen and me to have coffee with the Duke and Duchess of Sussex (that's Prince Harry and Meghan Markle) to discuss mental health, when they were on their New Zealand tour in 2018. I remember sitting on the phone, with Alex sitting opposite me, trying to keep calm and collected on the phone but signalling to Alex that I was being asked about the royals. It was so surreal, and when I hung up I just burst out laughing, going, 'What just happened?!'

When it got hard, I always clung onto the 'why'—knowing that it was

helping people and that they were finding hope kept me going.

In amongst the craziness of having coffee with royalty, I was also doing TEDx talks and getting nominated for awards like 'Young New Zealander of the Year'. It was all so crazy—it felt like a whirlwind.

While it was incredible, it was also a lot harder than people know. There were many nights that I wanted to quit being an advocate—when I was losing people all around me to suicide, on the phone to the police all the time telling them about people I thought were at risk, and getting stopped as I walked through the mall by people wanting to tell their stories. It was a lot to deal with, but when it got hard, I always clung onto that 'why'—knowing that it was helping people and that they were finding hope kept me going.

In March 2019, *Jessica's Tree* finally went out into the world. I was so anxious—this was what I had worked so hard on for the last two years. The film crew shooting the feature film were with me for 72 hours nonstop during the series release.

When I woke up the morning of 10 March 2019, my social media was already filled with messages from people who had seen the video in the early hours of the morning, immediately after it went live. A story about it was on the front page of the *New Zealand Herald,* and I had back-to-back media interviews all day.

Jessica's Tree went on to win awards all over the world, but beyond that recognition I just felt so incredibly amazed at the personal response to the series. People were loving it—many of them were finding hope, and others were feeling that they understood suicide and mental-health issues so much more.

Following the release of *Jessica's Tree,* more international opportunities opened up. Gen and I were invited to London to meet with The Royal Foundation and others. While we were there we also met with an incredible woman called Elisha London, the CEO of United for Global Mental Health. She started talking to us about this new global mental-health campaign they were working on, and asked us if we would be interested in representing New Zealand on it. Both Gen and I immediately knew this was something we wanted to do—hearing of Elisha's passion and determination to make change captivated us. We were also heartbroken to hear that every 40 seconds, someone, somewhere in the world dies through suicide.

It was during this conversation with Elisha that I realised how much of a global issue suicide and mental illness is. This wasn't a New Zealand issue, but a global one ... and if we wanted to make real change, then we had to begin to work together with other countries.

In August 2019, Gen and I flew to Indonesia to attend an Asia-Pacific workshop on this new campaign. The cool thing about this story is that we actually ended up in Indonesia with Dr Stephanie Taylor—remember her? The doctor who got me admitted into the ward for the last time? She is now on our team and helping us launch the

New Zealand strand of this new campaign.

Hope is real, and change is possible.

As I sit here writing this book, I am preparing to go and help launch this campaign, called 'Speak your Mind', at the UN General Assembly. This will be the first mental-health campaign of its kind, calling on leaders around the world to be accountable for focusing on and resourcing mental health.

*

If you told the three-year-old girl being sexually abused that one day she would tour the world, she would never have believed you. If you told the seven-year-old getting bullied, or the 12-year-old trying to take her own life; if you told the girl waking up from a coma or the girl sitting in the psych ward that one day she would become a voice for mental health and would be propelling change and helping launch the world's first global mental-health campaign, she would have laughed at you. If you told her that one day she would wake up so excited for life, that she would know what it is to be loved, that she would be surrounded by people who care and that one day she would know she was never a burden—well, she would have never seen that day coming. But it did.

My message to you is that you too can stop surviving and start fighting. There is always hope.

Dear Suicidal Me,

I know that right now the word 'hope' is just that — nothing more than a word. Right now it seems impossible, and you feel like you will be stuck in that way of thinking forever. But I promise you, you won't.

I know that your core belief is that you are unlovable, but trust me when I say look closer. There are people who love you unconditionally — they always have, but you just can't see it at the moment. Cling to the people who want the best for you and don't worry about the rest. At the end of the day it is going to be just those couple of people standing by your side in your darkest moments as they help guide you out.

You are not your abuse, you are not your past and you are not what your mind tells you. You are so much more than all of those things.

Oh yeah, and heads up: the word that meant nothing to you, 'hope' — well, you are going to be the co-founder of an entire organisation whose main goal is to speak hope. You will travel the world, touring high schools and confer-ences, sharing your story of how you persevered through the darkest times and came out on top.

You will gain a passion for telling people's stories, for creating documentaries and interviews that provoke change, and this will lead to you becoming the youngest funded documentary director in New Zealand. You will win awards all around the world. You will become a face of hope, and you will speak to hundreds of thousands of people sharing your story on all kinds of platforms. You will sign a feature-film deal, a series deal. You will do TED talks, speak with royals and government.

But more than all of these things you will do, you will learn what it is to be loved. You will finally be able to see that actually those closest to you really do care. You are not a burden and you are loved. You will finally discover who you are, and those late nights spent crying and planning the end of your life will soon turn into nights of planning hope-filled content, campaigns and talks. Nights spent hanging with your incredible friends and new-found family.

Hang in there. I promise breakthrough is right around the corner.

Hope is real, and change is possible.

I am proof.

All my love,

Your older self

Victor Ugo and I launch the Museum of Lost and Found Potential in London.

Hugging someone after an event.

Coffee with Harry and Meghan.

Gen and me in London.

Voices of Hope filming.

The extended adopted family.

Esther and me at TED Talks.

Speak Your Mind campaigners in Indonesia.

Acknowledgements

First and foremost I want to acknowledge God. For me, faith has become a huge part of my story and my life and I know that I would not be here today if it wasn't for him walking with me every step of the way.

To the person who has stuck by me the longest, and the reason that this book is able to be written; Esther Greenwood. Thank you for never being afraid to have the hard conversations, for loving me enough to teach me how to fight, for challenging me, refusing to let me go around in circles and for simply loving me. The entire concept of this book has come about because of you and your unwavering wisdom. Thank you for never giving up on me, and for now championing me as I get to be a part of changing the world.

Wayne and Libby Huirua, the people who stepped into parental roles for me. Thank you for showing me what consistent, unconditional love is, and for fighting for me both in the psych ward and alongside me now as I work hard to change the story with mental health. Thank you for loving me unconditionally and for teaching me that I am loved for who I am and not what I do—I will be forever thankful.

Genevieve Mora, my partner in crime, friend and co-founder of Voices of Hope. None of this would be in existence if it wasn't for you. You have been on this journey with me for a long time and it has been an honour to watch you grow and become the strong advocate you are today. Voices of Hope would not exist without you; you held the fort while I was writing this book and encouraged me every step of the way. You are changing the world, thank you.

To Sam and Kathy Monk, you lead with humility, grace, strength and determination and have taught me what it is to be a courageous leader. I will never be able to thank you enough for everything you do to champion our entire community, not just in New Zealand but also around the world. Thank you for creating a space where I could come back and feel loved, accepted and a part of something greater.

To my army of people, Grace, Maddie and Mez, for being consistent, loyal, fun and loving friends. I am so incredibly thankful for each of you, for the Saturday morning walks, laughs and well-needed breaks through this writing process. Each of you sat with me at different times, ensuring that I finished this book and for that, and your friendship, I could not be more thankful.

To Alex Reed and Cass Avery for believing in a young girl from film school and enabling me to tell a story that has gone on to create change around the world. Your hard work, dedication and perseverance in telling both *Jessica's Tree* and also *The Girl on the Bridge* is the reason that we get to reach so many people today, so thank you.

And finally, to the New Zealand Police: the respect, admiration and gratitude I have for you is uncountable. Your officers stepped in and physically saved my life many, many times. I made their jobs tough at times, but I am so thankful that in my literal darkest moments they were there to ensure I could live another day. A special thank you to Constable Campbell, who went above and beyond and showed me that even strangers can care.

It takes a community of people to turn a story around like mine. And so to all of you who have been part of my life, who have been there, championed me, cried with me and laughed with me, I say thank you. By ourselves we can achieve very little, but together, as a community, we can change the world.

Where to get help

1737, NEED TO TALK? – Free call or text. Need to talk? 1737 is free to call or text from any landline or mobile phone, 24 hours a day 7 days a week.

ANXIETY NEW ZEALAND – 0800 ANXIETY – (0800 269 4389)

DEPRESSION HELPLINE – 0800 111 757 or free text 4202 (to talk to a trained counsellor about how you are feeling or to ask any questions) (available 24/7)

HEALTHLINE – 0800 611 116

KIDSLINE – 0800 54 37 54 (0800 KIDSLINE) for young people up to 18 years of age (available 24/7)

LIFELINE – 0800 543 354 (0800 LIFELINE) or free text 4357 (HELP) (available 24/7)

PARENT HELP – 0800 568 856 for parents/whānau seeking support, advice and practical strategies on all parenting concerns. Anonymous, non-judgemental and confidential.

RAINBOW YOUTH – (09) 376 4155 available 11am–5pm weekdays.

RURAL SUPPORT TRUST – 0800 787 254

SAMARITANS – 0800 726 666 (available 24/7)

SHINE (DOMESTIC VIOLENCE) – 0508 744 633 available 9am–11pm, 7 days a week.

SKYLIGHT – 0800 299 100 for support through trauma, loss and grief; 9am–5pm weekdays.

SPARX.ORG.NZ – online e-therapy tool provided by the University of Auckland that helps young people learn skills to deal with feeling down, depressed or stressed.

SUICIDE CRISIS HELPLINE – 0508 828 865 (0508 TAUTOKO) a free, nationwide service available 24 hours a day, 7 days a week and is operated by highly trained and experienced telephone counsellors who have undergone advanced suicide prevention training.

SUPPORTING FAMILIES IN MENTAL ILLNESS – 0800 732 825

THELOWDOWN.CO.NZ – or email team @thelowdown.co.nz or free text 5626

WHAT'S UP – 0800 942 8787 (for 5–18 year olds). Phone counselling is available Monday to Friday, 12 noon–11pm and weekends, 3pm–11pm. Online chat is available from 1pm–10pm Monday to Friday, and 3pm–10pm on weekends.

WOMEN'S REFUGE – 0800 733 843 (0800 REFUGE) for women living with violence, or in fear, in their relationship or family.

WWW.DEPRESSION.ORG.NZ – includes The Journal online help service.

YOUTHLINE – Free call 0800 376 633, Free text 234, talk@youthline.co.nz

International

AUSTRALIA

LIFELINE – 13 11 14

KIDSLINE – 1800 55 1800

BEYOND BLUE – 1300 22 4636

USA

SUICIDE PREVENTION HELPLINE – 1 800 273 8255

CRISIS TEXT LINE – text HOME to 741741

UK

1 800 SUICIDE – 1 800 784 2433

1 800 273 TALK – 1 800 273 8255

UK SUICIDE HOTLINE – 08 457 90 90 90

CRISIS TEXT LINE – text 85258

CANADA

CRISIS SUPPORT – 1 833 456 4566

CRISIS TEXT LINE – text HOME to 686868

CPSIA information can be obtained
at www.ICGtesting.com
Printed in the USA
BVHW041146130521
607269BV00002B/462

9 780369 356802